The history of Oronooko; or, the royal slave. A novel. Containing a variety of entertaining passages. Published by Charles Gildon. The ninth edition corrected.

Aphra Behn

ECCO
PRINT EDITIONS

Eighteenth Century
Collections Online
Print Editions

Gale ECCO Print Editions

Relive history with *Eighteenth Century Collections Online*, now available in print for the independent historian and collector. This series includes the most significant English-language and foreign-language works printed in Great Britain during the eighteenth century, and is organized in seven different subject areas including literature and language; medicine, science, and technology; and religion and philosophy. The collection also includes thousands of important works from the Americas.

The eighteenth century has been called "The Age of Enlightenment." It was a period of rapid advance in print culture and publishing, in world exploration, and in the rapid growth of science and technology – all of which had a profound impact on the political and cultural landscape. At the end of the century the American Revolution, French Revolution and Industrial Revolution, perhaps three of the most significant events in modern history, set in motion developments that eventually dominated world political, economic, and social life.

In a groundbreaking effort, Gale initiated a revolution of its own: digitization of epic proportions to preserve these invaluable works in the largest online archive of its kind. Contributions from major world libraries constitute over 175,000 original printed works. Scanned images of the actual pages, rather than transcriptions, recreate the works *as they first appeared.*

Now for the first time, these high-quality digital scans of original works are available via print-on-demand, making them readily accessible to libraries, students, independent scholars, and readers of all ages.

For our initial release we have created seven robust collections to form one the world's most comprehensive catalogs of 18th century works.

Initial Gale ECCO Print Editions collections include:

History and Geography
Rich in titles on English life and social history, this collection spans the world as it was known to eighteenth-century historians and explorers. Titles include a wealth of travel accounts and diaries, histories of nations from throughout the world, and maps and charts of a world that was still being discovered. Students of the War of American Independence will find fascinating accounts from the British side of conflict.

Social Science

Delve into what it was like to live during the eighteenth century by reading the first-hand accounts of everyday people, including city dwellers and farmers, businessmen and bankers, artisans and merchants, artists and their patrons, politicians and their constituents. Original texts make the American, French, and Industrial revolutions vividly contemporary.

Medicine, Science and Technology

Medical theory and practice of the 1700s developed rapidly, as is evidenced by the extensive collection, which includes descriptions of diseases, their conditions, and treatments. Books on science and technology, agriculture, military technology, natural philosophy, even cookbooks, are all contained here.

Literature and Language

Western literary study flows out of eighteenth-century works by Alexander Pope, Daniel Defoe, Henry Fielding, Frances Burney, Denis Diderot, Johann Gottfried Herder, Johann Wolfgang von Goethe, and others. Experience the birth of the modern novel, or compare the development of language using dictionaries and grammar discourses.

Religion and Philosophy

The Age of Enlightenment profoundly enriched religious and philosophical understanding and continues to influence present-day thinking. Works collected here include masterpieces by David Hume, Immanuel Kant, and Jean-Jacques Rousseau, as well as religious sermons and moral debates on the issues of the day, such as the slave trade. The Age of Reason saw conflict between Protestantism and Catholicism transformed into one between faith and logic -- a debate that continues in the twenty-first century.

Law and Reference

This collection reveals the history of English common law and Empire law in a vastly changing world of British expansion. Dominating the legal field is the *Commentaries of the Law of England* by Sir William Blackstone, which first appeared in 1765. Reference works such as almanacs and catalogues continue to educate us by revealing the day-to-day workings of society.

Fine Arts

The eighteenth-century fascination with Greek and Roman antiquity followed the systematic excavation of the ruins at Pompeii and Herculaneum in southern Italy; and after 1750 a neoclassical style dominated all artistic fields. The titles here trace developments in mostly English-language works on painting, sculpture, architecture, music, theater, and other disciplines. Instructional works on musical instruments, catalogs of art objects, comic operas, and more are also included.

old books. new life.

The BiblioLife Network

This project was made possible in part by the BiblioLife Network (BLN), a project aimed at addressing some of the huge challenges facing book preservationists around the world. The BLN includes libraries, library networks, archives, subject matter experts, online communities and library service providers. We believe every book ever published should be available as a high-quality print reproduction; printed on-demand anywhere in the world. This insures the ongoing accessibility of the content and helps generate sustainable revenue for the libraries and organizations that work to preserve these important materials.

The following book is in the "public domain" and represents an authentic reproduction of the text as printed by the original publisher. While we have attempted to accurately maintain the integrity of the original work, there are sometimes problems with the original work or the micro-film from which the books were digitized. This can result in minor errors in reproduction. Possible imperfections include missing and blurred pages, poor pictures, markings and other reproduction issues beyond our control. Because this work is culturally important, we have made it available as part of our commitment to protecting, preserving, and promoting the world's literature.

GUIDE TO FOLD-OUTS MAPS and OVERSIZED IMAGES

The book you are reading was digitized from microfilm captured over the past thirty to forty years. Years after the creation of the original microfilm, the book was converted to digital files and made available in an online database.

In an online database, page images do not need to conform to the size restrictions found in a printed book. When converting these images back into a printed bound book, the page sizes are standardized in ways that maintain the detail of the original. For large images, such as fold-out maps, the original page image is split into two or more pages

Guidelines used to determine how to split the page image follows:

• Some images are split vertically; large images require vertical and horizontal splits.
• For horizontal splits, the content is split left to right.
• For vertical splits, the content is split from top to bottom.
• For both vertical and horizontal splits, the image is processed from top left to bottom right.

Ann Jason

her Book

0126'' ... 16.

THE
HISTORY

Ann OF *Fiason*

ORONOOKO;

OR, THE

ROYAL SLAVE.

Ann A *Fiason*

NOVEL.

CONTAINING

A variety of Entertaining PASSAGES.

PUBLISHED BY CHARLES GILDON.

The Ninth Edition corrected.

DONCASTER

Printed by C. PLUMMER, MDCCLXX.

THE

HISTORY

OF THE

ROYAL SLAVE.

I Do not pretend, in giving you the history of this Royal Slave to entertain my reader with the adventures of a feigned hero, whose life and fortunes fancy may manage at the poet's pleasure; nor in relating the truth, design to adorn it with any accidents, but such as arrived in earnest to him. and it shall come simply into the world, recommended by its own

proper

proper merits, and natural intrigues; there being enough of reality to suppose it, and to render it diverting, without the addition of invention.

I was myself an eye-witness to a great part of what you will find here set down; and what I could not be witness of, I receiv'd from the mouth of the chief actor in this history, the hero himself, who gave us the whole transactions of his youth; and I shall omit for brevity's sake, a thousand little incidents of his life, which however pleasant to us, where history was scarce, and adventures very rare, yet might prove tedious and heavy to the reader, in a world where he finds diversions for every minute, new and strange. But we who were perfectly charm'd with the character of this great man, were curious to gather every circumstance of his life.

The scene of the last part of his adventures lies in a colony in America, called Surinam, in the West-Indies.

But before I give you the story of this gallant slave, 'tis fit I tell you the manner of bringing them to these new colonies; those they make use of there, not being

natives

natives of the place; for those we live with in perfect amity, without daring to command 'em; but on the contrary, arefs 'em with all the brotherly and friendly affection in the world; trading with them for their fish, venison, buffaloe's-skins and little rarities; as marmosets, a fort of monkey, as big as a rat or weafel, but of a marvellous and delicate shape having face and hands like a human creature; and cousheries, a little beast in the form and fashion of a lion, as big as a kitten, but so exactly made in all parts like that noble beast, that it is it in miniature; then for little paraketoes, great parrots muckaws, and a thousand other birds and beasts of wonderful and surprizing forms, shapes and colours: for skins of prodigious snakes, of which there are some threescore yards in length; as is the skin of one that may be seen at his majesty's antiquary's; where are also some rare flies, of amazing forms and colours, presented to 'em by myself; some as big as my fist, some less; and all of various excellencies, such as art cannot imitate. Then we trade for feathers which

they

they order into all fhapes, make themfelves little fhort habits of 'em, and glorious wreaths for their heads, necks, arms
and legs, whofe tinctures are inconceiva-
ble. I had a fet of thefe prefented to me
and I gave 'em to the king's theatre, it
was the drefs of the Indian Queen, infinitely admired by perfons of quality, and
was inimitable. Befides thefe, a thoufand
little knacks, and rarities in nature, and
fome of art, as their bafkets, weapons, a-
prons, &c. We dealt with them with
beads of all colours, knives, axes, pins and
needles, which they ufed only as tools to
drill holes with in their ears, nofes, and
lips, where they hang a great many little
things ; as long beads, bits of tin, brafs or
filver beat thin, and any fhining trinket.
The beads they weave into an apron a-
bout a quarter of an ell long, and of the
fame breadth ; working them very pret-
tily in flowers of feveral colours, which
apron they wear juft before 'em, as Adam
and Eve did the fig -leaves ; the men wear-
ing a long ftripe of linen, which they deal
with us for. They thread thefe beads alfo on long cotton-threads, and make gir-

A 3   dles

dles to tie their ap ons to which come
twenty times or more about the waste,
and then cross, like a shoulder-belt, both
ways, and round t en necks, arms, and
legs. This adornment, with their long
black hair, and the face painted in little
specks or flowers here and there, make
'em a wonderful figure to behold. Some
of the beauties, which indeed are finely
shap'd, as almost all are, who have pretty features, are charming and novel; for
they have all that is called beauty, except
the colour, which is a reddish yellow;
or after a red oiling, which they often
use to themselves, they are of the colour
of a new brick but smooth, soft and sleek.
They are extreme modest and bashful,
very shy, and nice of being touch'd. And
tho' they are all thus naked if one lives
fo ever among 'em, there is not to be
feen an indecent action, or glance, and
being continually us'd to fee one another
fo unadorned, fo like our first parents before the fall. it seems as if they had no
wishes there being nothing to heighten
curiosity, but all you can fee, you fee
at once, and every moment fee; and

where

where there is no novelty, there can be no curiofity. Not but I have feen a hand-fome young indian, dying for love of a very beautiful young indian maid; but all his courtfhip was, to fold his arms, purfue her with his eyes, and fighs were all his language while fhe, as if no fuch lover were prefent, or rather if fhe defired none fuch, carefully guarded her eyes from beholding him; and never approached him, but fhe looked down with all the blufhing modefty I have feen in the moft fevere and cautious of our world. And thefe people reprefented to me an abfolute idea of the firft ftate of innocence, before man knew how to fin. and 'tis moft evident and plain, that fimple nature is the moft harmlefs, inoffenfive and virtuous miftrefs. 'Tis fhe alone, if fhe were permitted, that better inftructs the world, than all the inventions of man: religion would here but deftroy that tranquillity they poffefs by ignorance; and laws would but teach 'em to know offences, of which now they have no notion. They once made mourning and fafting for the death of the Englifh Governor,

A 4   who

who had given his hand to come on such a day to 'em, and neither came nor sent, believing, when a man's word was past, nothing but death could or should prevent his keeping it; and when they saw he was not dead they ask'd him what name they had for a man who promis'd a thing he did not do? The Governor told them such a man was a liar, which was a word of infamy to a gentlemen. Then one of 'em reply'd, 'Governor, you are a lyar, ' and guilty of that infamy.' They have a native justice, which knows no fraud; and they understand no vice, or cunning, but when they are taught by the white men They have Plurality of wives; which when they grow old, serve those that succeed 'em, who are young, but with a servitude easy and respected; and unless they take slaves in war, they have no other attendants.

Those on that continent where I was, had no King; but the oldest war-captain was obey'd with great resignation.

A war-captain is a man who has led them on to battle with conduct and success; of whom I shall have occasion to
speak

speak more hereafter, and of some other of their customs and manners, as they fall in my way.

With these people, as I said, we live in perfect tranquillity, and good understanding, as it behoves us to do; they knowing all the places where to seek the best food of the country, and the means of getting it, and for very small and unvaluable trifles, supplying us with what 'tis almost impossible for us to get; for they do not only in the woods, and over the savanah's, in hunting, supply the part of hounds, by swiftly scouring thro' those almost impassable places, and by the mere activity of their feet, run down the nimblest deer, and other eatable beasts; but in the water, one would think they were gods of the rivers, or fellow-citizens of the deep; so rare an art they have in swimming, diving, and almost living in water; by which they command the less swift inhabitants of the floods. And then for shooting, what they cannot take, or reach with their hands, they do with their arrows; and have so admirable an aim, that they will split almost an hair, and at

B 5

any

any diftance that an arrow can reach: they will fhoot down oranges, and other fruit, and only touch the ftalk with the dart's point, that tney may not hurt the fruit. So that they being on all occafions very ufeful to us, we find it abfolutely neceffary to carefs'em as friends, and not to treat'em as flaves, nor dare we do otherwife, their numbers fo far furpaffing ours on that continent.

Thofe then whom we make ufe of to work in our plantations of fugar, are negroes, black-flaves altogether, who are tranfported thither in this marner.

Thofe who want flaves, make a bargain with a mafter, or a captain of a fhip, and contract to pay him fo much a piece, a matter of twenty pounds a head, for as many as he agrees for, and to pay for 'em when they fhall be delivered on fuch a plantation; fo that when there arrives a fhip laden with flaves, they who have fo contracted, go aboard and receive their number by lot; and perhaps in one lot they may be for ten, there may happen to be three or four men, the reft women and children. Or be there more or lefs

of

of either fex, you are obliged to be contented with your lot.

Coramantien, a country of blacks fo called, was one of thofe places in which they found the moft advantageous trading for thefe flaves, and thither moft of our great traders in that merchandize traffic; for that nation is very warlike and brave; and having a continual campaign, being always in hoftilities with one neighbouring prince or other, they had the fortune to take a great many captives: for all they took in battle were fold as flaves, at leaft thofe common men who could not ranfom themfelves. Of thefe flaves fo taken, the general only has all the profit; and of thefe generals our captains and mafters of fhips buy all their freights.

The king of Coramantien was of himfelf a man of an hundred and odd years old, and had no fon, tho' he had many beautiful black wives; for moft certainly there are beauties that can charm of that colour. In his younger years he had had many gallant men to his fons, thirteen of whom died in battle, conquering when the fell; and he had only left him for his

A 6   fucsucceſſor, one grand-child, ſon to one of theſe dead victors, who, as ſoon as he could bear a bow in his hand, and a quiver at his back, was ſent into the field, to be trained up by one of the oldeſt generals to war; where, from his natural inclination to arms, and the occaſions given 'im, with the good conduct of the old general, he became, at the age of ſeventeen, one of the moſt expert captains, and braveſt ſoldiers that ever ſaw the field of Mars; ſo that he was ador'd as the wonder of all that world, and the darling of the ſoldiers. Beſides, he was adorned with a native beauty, ſo tranſcending all thoſe of his gloomy race, that he ſtruck an awe and reverence, even into thoſe that knew not his quality; as he did into me, who beheld him with ſurprize and wonder, when afterwards he arrived in our world.

He had ſcarce arrived at his ſeventeenth year, when, fighting by his ſide, the general was killed with an arrow in his eye, which the prince Oronooko [for ſo was the gallant moor called] very narrowly avoided; nor had he, if the general who

faw the arrow fhot, and perceiving it
aimed at the prince, had not bow'd his
head between, on purpofe to receive it
in his own body, rather than it fhould
touch that of the prince, and fo fav'd him

'Twas then, afflicted as Oroonoko was,
that he was proclaimed general in the old
man's place and then it was, at the fi-
nifhing of that war, which had continu'd
for two years, that the prince came to
court, where he had hardly been a month
together, from the time of his fifth year
to that of feventeen : and it was amazing
to imagine where it was he learned fo
much humanity, or to give his accom-
plifhments a greater name, where 'twas
he got that real greatnefs of foul, thofe
refined notions of true honour, and abfolute generofity. and that foftnefs, that
was capable of the higheft paffion of love
and gallantry, whofe objects were almoft
continually fighting men, or thofe mangled or dead, who heard no founds but
thofe of war and groans. Some part of
it we may attribute to the care of a
Frenchman of wit and learning, who finding it turn to a very good account to be

a fort of royal tutor to this young black, and perceiving him very ready, apt, and quick of apprehenfion, took a great pleature to teach him morals, language, and icience ; and was for it extremely belov'd and valu'd by him. Another reafon was, he lov'd when he came from war, to fee all the Englifh gentlemen that traded thither, and did not only learn their language but that of the Spaniards alfo, with whom he traded afterwards for flaves.

I have often feen and converfed with this great man, and been a witrefs to many of his mighty actions , and do affure my reader, the moft illuftrious courts could not have produced a braver man, both for greatnefs of courage and mind, a judgment more folid, a wit more quick, and a converfation more fweet and diverting. He knew almoft as much as if he had read much : He had heard of and admired the Romans ; he had heard of the late civil wars in England, and the deplorable death of our great monarch ; and would difcourfe of it with all the fenfe and abhorrence of the injuftice imaginable. He had an extreme good and graceful

mien

mien, and all the civility of a well-bred great man. He had nothing of barbarity in his nature, but to all points addressed himself as if his education had been in some European court.

This great and just character of Oroonoko gave me an extreme curiosity to see him, especially when I knew he spoke French and English, and that I could talk with him. But tho' I had heard so much of him I was as greatly surprized when I saw him, as if I had heard nothing of him; so beyond all report I found him. He came into the room, and addressed himself to me, and some other woman, with the best grace in the world. He was pretty tall, but of a shape the most exact that can be fancied ; the most famous statuary, could not form the figure of a man more admirably turn'd from head to foot. His face was not of that brown rusty black, which most of that nation are, but a perfect ebony, or polished jet. His eyes were the most awful that could be seen, and very piercing ; the white of 'em being like snow, as were his teeth. His nose was rising and Roman, instead of African

and

and flat : his mouth the fineft fhaped that
could be feen, far from thofe great turn'd
Lips, which are fo natural to the reft of
the negroes. The whole proportion and
air of his face was fo nobly and exactly
form'd, that bating his colour, there
cou'd be nothing in nature more beautiful, agreeable, and handfome. There
was no one grace wanting, that bears the
ftandard of true beauty. His hair came
down to his fhoulders, by the aids of art,
which was by pulling it out with a quill,
and keeping it comb'd, of which he took
particular care. Nor did the perfections
of his mind come fhort of thofe of his
perfon, for his difcourfe was admirable
upon almoft any fubject ; and whoever
had heard him fpeak, would have been
convinced of their errors, that all fine
wit is confined to the white men efpecially to thofe of Chriftendom ; and would
have confeffed that Oronooko was as capable even of reigning well, and of go-
verning as wifely, had as great a foul, as
politick maxims, and was as fenfible of
power, as any prince civilized in the moft
refin'd fchools of humanity and learning,
or the moft illuftrious courts.

This prince, such as I have described him, whose soul and body were so admirably adorned, was [while yet he was in the court of his grandfather, as I said] as capable of love, as 'twas possible for a brave and gallant man to be ; and in saying that, I have named the highest degree of love ; for sure great souls are most capable of that passion.

I have already said, the old general was killed by the shot of an arrow, by the side of this prince, in battle ; and that Oronooko was made general. This old dead hero had one only daughter left of his race, a beauty, that to describe her truly, one need only say, she was female to the noble male ; the beautiful black Venus to our young Mars ; as charming in her person as he, and of delicate virtues. I have seen a hundred white men sighing after her, and making a thousand vows at her feet, all in vain and unsuccessful, and she was indeed too great for any but a prince of her own nation to adore.

Oronooko coming from the wars, (which were now ended) after he had made his court to his grandfather, he

A 9   thought

thought in honour he ought to make a
visit to Imonda, the daughter of his foster
father, the dead general ; to make some
excuses to her, because his preservation
was the occasion of her father's death ;
and to present her with those slaves that
had been taken in this last battle, as the
trophies of her father's victories. When
he came, attended by all the young soldiers of any merit, he was infinitely surprized at the beauty of this fair queen of
night, whose face and person were so far
exceeding all he ever beheld, that lovely
modesty with which she received him,
that softness in her looks and sighs, upon
the melancholy occasion of this honour
that was done her by so great a man as
Oroonoko, and a prince of whom she had
heard such admirable things , the awe-
fulness wherewith she received him, and
the sweetness of her words and behaviour
while he stay'd, gain'd a perfect conquest
over his fierce heart, and made him feel
the victor could be subdu'd. So that having made his first compliments, and presented her an hundred and fifty slaves in
fetters, he told her with his eyes, that he

was

was not infenfible of her charms; while
Imoinda, who wifh'd for nothing more
than fo glorious a conqueft, was pleafed
to believe, that fhe underftood that filent
language of new born love ; and, from
that moment, put on all her additions to
beauty.

The prince return'd to court with quite
another honour than before ; and though
he did not fpeak much of the fair Imoindà
he had the pleafure to hear all his follow-
ers fpeak of nothing but the charms of
that maid; infomuch, that, even in the
prefence of the old king, they were ex-
tolling her, and heightning if poffible the
beauties they had found in her: fo that
nothing elfe was talk'd of, no other found
was heard in every corner where there
were whifperers, but Imoinda! Imoinda!

"Twill be imagined Oronooko ftayed
not long before he made his fecond vifit;
nor, confidering his quality, not much
longer before he told her, he ador'd her.
I have often heard him fay, that he admired by what ftrange infpiration he came
to talk things fo foft and fo paffionate,
who never knew love, nor was us'd to the
converfation

converfation of women; but [to ufe his own words] he faid, 'moft happily, fome 'new. and, till then, unknown power, in-'ftructed his heart and tongue in the lan-'guage of love, and at the fame time, 'in favour of him, infpired Iominda with 'a fenfe of his paffion.' She was touch'd with what he faid, and return'd it all in fuch anfwers as went to his very heart, with a pleafure unknown before. Nor dd he ufe thofe obligations ill, that love had done him, he turn'd all his happy moments to the beft advantage; and as he knew no vice, his flame aim'd at nothing but honour, if fuch a diftinction may be made in love; and efpecially in that country, where men take to themfelves as many as they can mantain; and where the only crime and fin againft a woman, is to turn her off, to abandon her to want, fhame and mifery · fuch ill morals are only practifed in chriftian countries, where they pefer the bare name of religion; and, without virtue or morality, think that fufficient. But Oronooko was none of thofe profeffors; but as he had right notions of honour, fo he made her fuch

propofitions

propofitions as were not only and barely fuch, but, contrary to the cuftom of his country, he made her vows, fhe fhould be the only woman he would poffefs while he liv'd ; that no age or wrinkles fhould incline him to change. for her foul would be always fine, and always young; and he fhould have an eternal idea in his mind of the chaims fhe now bore ; and fhould look into his heart for that idea, when he could find it no longer in her face.

After a thoufand affurances of his lafting flames, and her eternal empire over him, fhe condefcended to receive him for her hufband ; or rather, receive him as the greateft honour the gods could do her.

There is a certain ceremony in thefe cafes to be obferv'd which I forgot to afk how 'twas perform'd ; but 'twas concluded on both fides, that in obedience to him, the grandfather was to be firft made acquainted with the defign · for they pay a moft abfolute refignation to the monarch, efpecially when he is a parent alfo.

On the other fide, the old king, who had many wives, and many concubines, wanted not court flatterers to infinuate

into

into his heart a thousand tender thoughts for this young beauty ; and who represented her to his fancy, as the most charming he had ever possess'd in all the long race of his numerous years. At this character, his old heart, like an extinguish'd brand, most apt to take fire felt new sparks of love, and began to kindle ; and now grown to his second childhood, long'd with impatience to behold this gay thing, with whom, alas! he could but innocently play. But how he should be confirm'd she was this wonder before he us'd his power to call her to court, [where maidens never came unless for the king's private use] he was next to consider; and while he was so doing, he had intelligence brought him, that Imoinda was most certainly mistress to the prince Oroonoko. This gave him some chagrin : however it gave him also an opportunity, one day when the prince was a hunting, to wait on a man of quality, as his slave and attendant, who should go and make a present to Imoinda, as from the the prince ; he should then unknown, see this fair maid, and have an opportunity to hear what message she

would

would return the prince for his prefent,
and from thence gather the ftate of her
heart, and degree of her inclination.——
This was put in execution, and the old
monarch faw, and burn'd : he found her
all he had heard, and would not delay
his happinefs, but found he fhould have
fome obftacle to overcome her heart ; for
fhe exprefled her fenfe of the prefent the
prince had fent her, in terms fo fweet,
fo foft and pretty, with an air of love and
joy that could not be diffembled, infomuch that 'twas paft doubt whether fhe
lov'd Oroonoko entirely. This gave the
old king fome affliction, but he falv'd it
with this, that the obedience the people
pay their king, was not at all inferior to
what they paid their gods ; and what
love could not oblige Imoinda to do,
duty would compel her to.

He was therefore no fooner got 'into
his apartment, but he fent the royal veil
to Imoinda, that is the ceremony of in-
vitation ; he fends the lady he has a mind
to honour with his bed, a veil with which
fhe is covered, and fecured for the king's
ufe ; and 'tis death to difobey ; befides
a moft impious difobedience.

'Tis not to be imagined the furprize and grief that feiz'd the lovely maid at this news and fight. However as delays in thefe cafes are dangerous, and pleading worfe than treafon; trembling, and almoft fainting, fhe was obliged to fuffer herfelf to be covered, and led away

They brought her thus to court; and the king who had caufed a very rich bath to be prepar'd, was led into it, where he fat under a canopy, in ftate, to receive this long'd for virgin; whom he having commanded to be brought to him, they [after difrobing her] led her to the bath, and making faft the doors, left her to defcend. The king without more courtfhip, bad her throw off her mantle, and come to his arms; but Imoinda all in tears, threw herfelf on the marble on the brink of the bath, and befought him to hear her. She told him as fhe was a maid, how proud of the divine glory fhe fhould have been, of having it in her power to oblige her king; but as by the laws he could not, and from his royal goodnefs would not take from any man his wedded wife; fo fhe believed fhe
fhould

should be the occasion of making him commit a great sin, if she did not reveal her state and condition; and tell him she was another's, and could not be so happy to be his.

The king, enrag'd at this delay, hastily demanded the name of the bold man, that had married a woman of her degree, without his consent. Imoinda seeing his eyes fierce, and his hands tremble, (whether with age or anger, I knew not, but she fancy'd the last) almost repented she had said so much, for now she fear'd the storm would fall on the prince; she therefore said a thousand things to appease the raging of his flame, and to prepare him to hear who it was with calmness. but before she spoke, he imagn'd who she meant but would not seem to do so, but commanded her to lay aside her mantle, and suffer herself to receive his caresses, or, by his Gods he swore, that happy man whom she was going to name should die, tho' it were even Oroonoko himself.— Therefore, (said he) deny this marriage, and swear thyself a maid. That (reply'd Imoinda) by all our powers I do; for I

am

am not yet known to my hufband. 'Tis enough, faid the king, 'tis enough, both to fatisfy my confcience and my heart.— And rifing from his feat, he went and led her into the bath ; it being in vain to refift.

In this time, the prince who was returnd from hunting, went to vifit his Imoinda, but found her gone ; and not only fo, but heard fhe had receiv'd the royal veil. This rais'd him to a ftorm ; and in his madnefs, they had much to do to fave him from laying violent hands on himfelf. Force firft prevail'd and then reafon : they urg'd all to him that might oppofe his rage · but nothing weigh'd fo greatly with him as the king's old age, incapable of injuring him with Imoinda. He would give way to that hope, becaufe it pleas'd him moft, and flatter'd beft his heart. Yet this ferv'd not altogether to make him ceafe his different paffions, which fometimes rag'd within him and foftened into fhowers. 'Twas not enough to appeafe him, to tell him his grandfather was old, and could not that way injure him, while he retained

that

that awful duty which the young men are us'd there to pay to their grave relations. He could not be convinced he had no caufe to figh and mourn for the lofs of a miftrefs, he could not with all his ftrength and courage retrieve, and he would often cry, ' Oh, my friends ! were fhe in wall'd
' cities, or confined from me in fortifica-
' tions of the greateft ftrength ; did in-
' chantments or monfters detain her from
' me, I would venture thro' any hazard
' to free her · But here in the arms of
' a feeble old man, my youth, my vio-
' lent love, my trade in arms, and all
' my vaft defire of glory, avail me no-
' thing. Imoinda is as irrecoverably loft
' to me, as if fhe were fnatch'd by the
' cold arms of death Oh ! fhe is never
' to be retrieved. If I would wait tedious
' years, till fate fhould bow the old king
' to his grave, even that would not leave
' me Imoinda free ; but ftill that cuftom
' that makes it fo vile a crime for a fon
' to marry his father's wives or miftref-
' fes, would hinder my happinefs, unlefs
' I would either ignobly fet an ill prefi-
' dent to my fuccefſors, or abandon my
country

' country, and fly with her to fome un-
' known woild who never heard our
' ftory.'

But it was objected to him, that his
cafe was not the fame ; for Imoinda being his lawful wife by folemn contract,
'twas he was the injur'd man, and might
if he fo pleas'd, take Imoinda back, the
breach of the law being on his grandfather's fide ; and that if he could cir-
cumvent him, and redeem her from the
Otan, which is the palace of the king's
women, a fort of Seraglio, it was both
juft and lawful for him fo to do.

This reafoning had fome force upon
him, and he fhould have been entiyely
comforted, but for the thought that fhe
was poffeffed by his grandfather. However, he lov'd her fo well, that he was
refolve to believe what moft favoured
his hope, and to endeavour to learn from
Imoinda's own mouth, what only fhe
could fatisfy him in, whether fhe was
robb'd of that bleffing which was only
due to his faith and love. But as it was
very hard to get a fight of the women
(for no man ever enteied into the Otan

but

but when the king went to entertain himfelf with fome one of his wives or miftreffes; and 'twas death at any other
time, for any other to go in) fo he knew
not how to contrive to get a fight of her.

While Oroonoko felt all the agonies of
love, and fuffered under a torment the
moft painful in the world, the old king
was not exempted from his fhare of affliction. He was troubled, for having been
forced, by an irrefiftible paffion, to rob his
fon of a treafure, he knew, could not but
be extremely dear to him; fince fhe was
the moft beautiful that ever had been feen
and had befides, all the fweetnefs and
innocence of youth and modefty, with a
charm of wit furpaffing all. He found
that however fhe was forc'd to expofe her
lovely perfon to his wither'd arms, fhe
could only figh and weep there, and think
of Oroonoko; and oftentimes could not
forbear fpeaking of him, tho' her life
were by cuftom forfeited, by owning her
paffion. But fhe fpoke not of a lover
only, but of a prince dear to him to
whom fhe fpoke; and of the praifes of a
man, who, 'till now, fill'd the old man's
foul

foul with joy at every recital of his bravery, or even his name. And 'twas this
dotage on our young hero, that gave Imoinda a thoufand privileges to fpeak of him
without offending; and this condefcenfion
in the old king, that made her take the
fatisfaction of fpeaking of him fo very
often.

Befides, he many times enquired how
the prince bore himfelf; and thofe of
whom he afk'd, being entirely flaves to
the merits and virtues of the prince, ftill
anfwered what they thought conduced beft
to his fervice; which was, to make the
old king fancy that the prince had no
more intereft in Imoinda, and had refign'd
her willingly to the pleafure of the king·
that he diverted himfelf with his mathe-
maticians his fortifications, his officers,
and his hunting.

This pleas'd the old lover, who failed
not to report thefe things again to Imoinda, that fhe might, by the example of
her young lover, withdraw her heart, and
reft better contented in his arms. But
however fhe was forced to receive this
unwelcome news, in all appearances, with
unconcern

unconcern and content; her heart was burfting within, and fhe was only happy when fhe could get alone to vent her grief and moans with fighs and tears.

What reports of the prince's conduct were made to the king, he thought good to juftify, as far as poffibly he could, by his actions; and when he appeared in the prefence of the king, he fhewed a face not at all betraying his heart: fo that in a little time, the old man being entirely convinced that he was no longer a lover of Imoinda, he carried him with him into his train, to the Otan, often to banquet with his miftreffes. But as foon as he entered one day, into the apartment of Imoinda, with the king, at the firft glance from her eyes, notwithftanding all his determined refolution, he was ready to fink in the place where he ftood; and had certainly done fo, but for the fupport of Aboan, a young man who was next to him; which, with his change of countenance, had betrayed him, had the king chanced to look that way. And I have obferved, it is a very great error in thofe who laugh when one fays, a negro can change colour
lour

lours; for I have feen 'em as frequently blufh, and look pale, and that I faw as vifibly as ever I faw in the moft beautiful white. And 'tis certain, that both thefe changes were evident, this day in both thefe lovers. And Imoinda, who faw with fome joy the change in the prince's face, and found it in her own, ftrove to divert the king from beholding either, by a forc'd carefs with which fhe met him; which was a new wound in the heart of the poor dying prince. But as foon as the king was bufied in looking on fome fine thing of Imoinda's making, fhe had time to tell the prince with her angry but love-darting eyes, that fhe refented his coldnefs, and bemoan'd her own miferable captivity. Nor were his eyes lefs filent, but anfwered hers again, as much as eyes could do, inftructed by the moft tender and moft paffionate heart that ever lov'd: and they fpoke fo well, and fo effectually, as Imoinda no longer doubted but fhe was the only delight and darling of that foul fhe found pleading in him its right of love, which none was more willing to refign than fhe. And 'twas
this

this powerful language alone that in an inftant conveyed all the thoughts of their fouls to each other; that they both found there wanted but opportunity to make them both entirely happy. But when he faw another door opened by Onahal (a former old wife of the king's who now had charge of Imoinda) and faw the profpect of a bed of ftate made ready, with fweets and flowers for the dalliance of the king, who immediately led the trembling victim from his fight, into that prepared repofe; what rage! what wild frenzies feized his heart! which forcing to keep within bounds, and to fuffer without noife, it became the more infupportable, and rent his foul with ten thoufand pains. He was forc'd to retire to vent his groans where he fell down on a carpet, and lay ftruggling a long time, and only breathing now and then, —O Imoinda! When Onahal had finifhed her neceffary affairs within, fhutting the door, fhe came forth, to wait till the king called; and hearing fome one fighing in the other room, fhe paffed on, and found the prince in that deplorable condition,

which

which she thought needed her aid. She
gave him cordials, but all in vain; till
finding the nature of his disease, by his
sighs, and naming Imoinda, she told him
had not so much cause as he imagined to
afflict himself for if he knew the king so
well as she did, he would not loose a moment in jealousy; and that she was con-
fident that Imoinda bore, at this minute,
part in his affliction. Aboan was of the
same opinion, and both together persuaded him to re-assume his courage; and all
fitting down on the carpet, the prince
said so many obliging things to Onahal,
that he half persuaded her to be of his party; and she promised him, she would
thus far comply with his just desires, that
she would let Imoinda know how faith-
ful he was, what he suffered, and what
he said.

This discourse lasted till the king called,
which gave Oroonoko a certain satisfaction, and with the hope Onahal had made
him conceive, he assumed a look as gay
as 'twas possible a man in his circum-
stances could do, and presently after, he
was called with the rest who waited without.

out The king commanded Mufic to be brought, and feveral of his young wives and miftreffes came all together by his command, to dance before him; where Imoinda performed her part with an air and grace as much furpaffing all the reft as her beauty was above 'em, and received the prefent ordained as a prize. The prince was every moment more charmed with the new beauties and graces he beheld in the fair one; and while he gazed and fhe danced, Onahal was retired to a window with Aboan.

This Onahal, as I faid, was one of the caft miftreffes of the old king; and 'twas thefe [now paft their beauty] that was made guardians or governantes to the new and the young ones, and whofe bufinefs it was to teach them all thofe wanton arts of love, with which they prevailed and charmed heretofore in their turn; and who now treated the triumphing happy ones with all the feverity, as to liberty and freedom, that was poffible, in revenge of the honours they rob them of; envying them thofe fatisfactions, thofe gallantries and prefents, that were once

made

made to themselves, while youth and beauty lasted, and which they now saw pass as it were regardless by, and paid only to the blooming. And certainly nothing is more afflicting to a decayed beauty, than to behold in itself declining charms, that were once adored ; and to find those caresses paid to new beauties, to which once she laid claim; to hear them whisper as she passes by, that once was a delicate woman. Those abandon'd ladies therefore endeavour to revenge all the despights and decays of time on these flourishing happy ones. And 'twas this severity that gave Oroonoko a thousand fears he should never prevail with Onahal to see Imoinda. But, as I said, she was now retired to a window with Aboan.

This young man was not only one of the best quality, but a man extremely well made, and beautiful; and coming often to attend the king to the Otan, he had subdued the heart of the antiquated Onahal, which had not forgot how pleasant it was to be in love. And tho' she had some decays in her face, she had none in her sense and wit ; she was there agreeable

agreeable ftill even to Aboan's youth· fo that he took pleafure in entertaining her with difcourfes of love. He knew alfo, that to make his court to thefe fhe-favourites was the way to be great ; thefe being the perfons that do all affairs and bufinefs and court. He had alfo obferved, that fhe had given him glances more tender and inviting than fhe had done to others of his quality. And now, when he faw that her favour could fo abfolutely oblige the prince, he failed not to figh in her ear, and look with his eyes all foft upon her, and gave her hope that fhe had made fome impreffion on his heart. He found her pleafed at this, and making a thoufand advances to him, but the ceremony ending, and the king departing broke up the company for that day, and his converfation.

Aboan failed not that night to tell the prince of his fuccefs, and how advantageous the fervice of Onahal might be to his amour with Imoinda. The prince was overjoyed at this good news, and befought him if it were poffible, to carefs her fo, as to engage her entirely, which

B

ac

he could not fail to do, if he complied
with her defires for then [faid the prince]
her life lying at your mercy, fhe muft
grant you the requeft you make in my
behalf. Aboan underftood him and affured him he would make love fo effectually, that he would defy the moft expert miftrels of the art. to find out whether he diffembled it, or had it really.—
And 'twas with impatience they waited
the next opportunity of going to the
Otan.

The wars came on, the time of taking
the field approached ; and 'twas impoffi-
for the prince to delay his going at the
head of his army to encounter the enemy,
fo that every day feemed a tedious year,
till he faw his Imoinda for he believed
he could not live, if he were forced a-
way without being fo happy. 'Twas
with impatience therefore that he expected the next vifit the king would make;
and, according to his wifh, it was not
long.

The parley of the eyes of thefe two
lovers had not paffed fo fecretly, but an
old jealous lover could fpy it ; or rather,
he

he wanted not flatterers who told him they obferved it : fo that the prince was haftened to the camp, and this was the laft vifit he found he fhould make to the Otan ; he therefore urged Aboan to make the beft of this laft effort, and to explain himfelf fo to Onahal, that fhe deferring her enjoyment of her young lover no longer, might make way for the prince to fpeak to Imoinda.

The whole affair being agreed on between the prince and Aboan, they attended the king, as the cuftom was, to the Otan ; where, while the whole company was taken up in beholding the dancing, and antick poftures the women royal made to divert the king, Onahal fingled out Aboan, whom fhe found moft phable to her wifh. When fhe had him where fhe believed fhe could not be heard, fhe fighed to him, and foftly cry'd, 'Ah A-
' boan ! when will you be fenfible of my
' paffion ? I confefs it with my mouth,
' becaufe I would not give my eyes the
' lye ; and you have but too much alrea-
' dy perceived they have confeffed my
' flame ; nor would I have you believe,

' that,

‘ that becaufe I am the abandoned mif-
‘ trefs of a king, I efteem myfelf altoge-
‘ ther divefted of charms : no, Aboan ;
‘ I have ftill a reft of beauty enough en-
‘ gaging, and have learned to pleafe too
‘ well, not to be defirable. I can have
‘ lovers ftill, but will have none but A-
‘ boan Madam, replied the half-feign-
‘ ing youth ; you have already, by my
‘ eyes, found you can ftill conquer ; and
‘ I believe, 'tis in pity of me you con-
‘ defcend to the kind confeffion. But
‘ madam, words are ufed to but fo fmall
‘ a part of our country courtfhip, that
‘ 'tis rare one can get fo happy an op-
‘ portunity as to tell one's heart ; and
‘ thofe few minutes we have, are forced
‘ to be fnatched for more certain proofs
‘ of love than fpeaking and fighing; and
‘ fuch I languifh for.’

He fpoke with fuch a tone, that fhe
hoped it true, and could not forbear believing it ; and being wholly tranfported
with joy for having fubdued the fineft
of all the king's fubjects to her defires,
fhe took from her ears two large pearls,
and commanded him to wear 'em in his.

He

He would have refused them, crying. madam, thefe are not the proofs of your love that I expect ; 'tis opportunity, 'tis a lone hour only, that can make me happy. But forcing the pearls into his hand fhe whifpered foftly to him ; Oh ! do not fear a woman's invention. when love fets her a thinking. And prefling his hand, fhe cry'd, This night you fhall be happy. Come to the gate of the orange grove, behind the Otan, and I will be ready about midnight to receive you. 'Twas thus agreed, and fhe left him, that no notice might be taken of their fpeaking together.

The ladies were ftill dancing. and the king laid on a carpet. with a great deal of pleafure was beholding them, efpecially Imoinda, who that day appeared more lovely than ever, being enlivened with the good tidings Onahal had brought her, of the conftant paffion the prince had for her. The prince was laid on another carpet at the other end of the room, with his eyes fixed on the object of his foul ; and as fhe turned or moved, fo did they. and fhe alone gave his eyes and foul their

motions.

motions. Nor did Imoinda employ her eyes to any other ufe, than in beholding with infinite pleafure the joy fhe produc-ed in thofe of the prince. But while fhe was more regarding him than the fteps fhe took, fhe chanced to fall, and fo near him, as that leaping with extreme force from the carpet, he caught her in his arms as fhe fell ; and 'twas vifible to the whole prefent, the joy wherewith he re-ceived her. He clafped her clofe to his bofom, and quite forgot that reverence that was due to the miftrefs of a king, and that punifhment that is the reward of a boldnefs of this nature. And had not the prefence of mind of Imoinda, fonder of his fafety than her own, befriended him, in making a fpring from his arms, and fell into her dance again, he had at that inftant met his death ; for the old king, jalous to the laft degree, rofe up in a rage, broke up the diverfion and led Imoinda to her apartment, fent out word to the prince, to go immediately to the camp ; and that if he were found another night in court, he fhould fuffer the death ordained for difobedient offenders.

You

You may imagine how welcome this news was to Oroonoko, whose unseasonable transport and caress of Imoinda was blamed by all men that loved him ; and now he perceived his fault, yet cried, that for such another moment he would be content to die.

All the Otan was in disorder about this accident ; and Onahal was particularly concerned, because on the prince's stay depended her happiness ; for she could no longer expect that of Aboan · so that e'er they departed, they contrived it so, that the prince and he should both come that night to the grove of the Otan, which was all of oranges and citrons, and that there they would wait her orders.

They parted thus with grief enough 'till night, leaving the king in possession of the lovely maid. But nothing could appease the jealousy of the old lover, he would not be imposed on, but would have it, that Imoinda made a false step, on purpose to fall into Oroonoko's bosom, and that all things looked like a design on both sides ; and 'twas in vain she protested her innocence : he was old

B 4   and

and obstinate, and left her more than half assured that his fear was true.

The king going to his apartment, sent to know where the prince was, and if he intended to obey his command. The messenger returned, and told him he found the prince pensive, and altogether unprepared for the campaign; that he lay negligently on the ground, and answered very little. This confirmed the jealousy of the king, and he commanded that they should very narrowly and privately watch his motions; and that he should not stir from his apartment, but one way or other should be employed to watch him; so that the hour approaching wherein he was to go to the citron-grove, and taking only Aboan along with him him, he leaves his apartment and was watched to the very gate of the Otan; where he was seen to enter, and where they left him, to carry back the tidings to the king.

Oroonoko and Aboan were no sooner entered, but Onahal led the prince to the apartment of Imoinda; who not knowing any thing of her happiness, was laid

in bed. But Onahal only left him in her
chamber, to make the best of his opportunity, and took her dear Aboan to her
own; where he shewed the height of
complaisance for his prince, when to give
him an opportunity, he suffered himself
to be caressed in bed by Onahal.

The prince softly awaked Imoinda,
who was not a little surprized with joy
to find him there; and yet she trembled
with a thousand fears. I believe he o-
mitted saying nothing to this young maid
that might persuade her to suffer him to
seize his own, and the rights of love.
And I believe she was not long resisting
those arms where she so longed to be;
and having opportunity, night and silence
youth, love, and desire, he soon prevail'd
and ravished in a moment what his old
grandfather had been endeavouring for
so many months

'Tis not to be imagined the satisfaction of these two lovers; nor the vows
she made him, that she remain'd a
spotless maid till that night. And that
what she did with his grandfather had
rob'd her of no part of her virgin hon-

B 5   our

our, the Gods in mercy and juftice, having referved that for her plighted lord,
to whom of right it belong'd. And 'tis
impoffible to exprefs the tranfports he
fuffered, while he liftened to a difcourfe
fo charming from her loved lips ; and
claired that body in his arms, for whom
he had fo long languifhed; and nothing
now afflicted him but his fudden depar-
ture from her ; for he told her the ne-
ceffity, and his commands, but fhould depart fatisfied in this, that fince the old
king had hitherto not been able to deprive him of thofe enjoyments which only belonged to him, he believed for the
future he would be lefs able to injure
him ; fo that abating the fcandal of the
veil, which was no otherwife fo, than that
fhe was wife to another, he believed her
fafe, even in the arms of the king and innocent ; yet would he have ventured at
the conqueft of the world, and have given
it all to have had her avoided that honour
of receiving the royal veil. 'Twas thus,
between a thoufand careffes, that both
bemoan'd that hard fate of youth and
beauty, fo liable to that cruel promotion;

'twas

'twas a glory that could well have been spared here, tho' desired and aim'd at by all the young females of that kingdom.

But while they were thus fondly employ'd, forgetting how time ran on, and that the dawn must conduct him far away from his only happiness, they heard a great noise in the Otan and unusual voices of men, at which the prince, starting from the arms of the frighted Imoinda, ran to a little battle-ax he used to wear by his side; and having not so much leisure as to put on his habit, he opposed himself against some who were already opening the door, which they did with so much violence, that Oroonoko was not able to defend it; but was forced to cry out with a commanding voice, 'Whoever 'ye are that have the boldness to at- 'tempt to approach this apartment thus 'rudely, know, that I, the prince O- 'roonoko, will revenge it with the cer- 'tain death of him that first enters, there- 'fore stand back, and know, this place 'is sacred to love and me this night; to- 'morrow 'tis the king's.'

This

This he spoke with a voice so resolved and assured, that they soon retired from the door, but cry'd, " 'Tis by the king's ' command we are come, and being sa-' tisfied by thy voice, O prince, as much ' as if we had entered, we can report ' to the king the truth of all his fears, ' and leave thee to provide for thy own ' safety, as thou art advised by thy own ' friends.

At these words they departed, and left him to take a short and sad leave of his mistress, who trusting in the strength of her charms, believed she should appease the fury of a jealous king, by saying she was surprized, and that it was by force he got into her apartment. All her concern now was for his life, and therefore she hastened him to the camp, and with much ado prevailed on him to go. Nor was it she alone that prevailed, Aboan and Onahal both pleaded, and both assured him of a lye that should be well enough contrived to secure Imoinda. So that at last, with a heart sad as death, dying eyes and sighing soul, Oroonoko departed, and took his way to the camp.

It

It was not long after, the king in perfon came to the Otan ; where, beholding
Imoinda, with rage in his eyes, he up-
braided her wickednefs and perfidy ; and
threatning her royal lover, fhe fell on
her face at his feet, bedewing the floor
with her tears, and imploring his pardon
for a fault, which fhe had not with her
will committed ; as Onahal who was alfo proftrate with her could teftify ; that
unknown to her, he had broke into her
apartment, and ravifhed her. She fpoke
this much againft her confcience, but to
fave her own life, 'twas abfolutely neceffary fhe fhould feign this falfity. She
knew it could not injure the prince. he
being fled to an army that would ftand
by him, againft any injuries that fhould
affault him. However, this laft thought
of Imoinda's being ravifhed, changed the
meafures of his revenge ; and whereas
before he defigned to be himfelf her executioner, he now refolved fhe fhould not
die. But as it is the greateft crime in
nature amongft them, to touch a women
after having been poffeffed by a fon, a
father, or a brother, fo now he looked

on

on Imoinda as a polluted thing wholly
unfit for his embraces; nor would he refign her to his grandfon, because she had
received the royal veil ; he therefore re-
moves her from the Otan, with Onahal ;
whom he put into fafe hands, with order
they should be both fold off as flaves to
another country, either christian or heathen, 'twas no matter where.

This cruel fentence, worse than death,
she implored might be reverfed; but
their prayers were vain, and it was put
in execution accordingly, and that with
fo much fecrecy, that none either without
or within the Otan, knew any thing of
their abfence, or their country.

The old king neverthelefs executed this
with a great deal of reluctancy ; but he
believed he had made a very great conqueft over himfelf, when he had once refolved. He believed now his love had
been unjuft; and that he could not expect the gods or captains of the clouds
[as they call the unknown powers] would
fuffer a better confequence from fo ill a
caufe. He now begins to hold Oroonoko
____ ____ ____ __ __ y he had reafon for

what

. And now every body could
.. .ing how paffionately Imoinda
was beloved by the prince; even thofe
confeffed it now, who faid the contrary
before his flame was not abated. So that
the king being old, and not being able
to defend himfelf in war, and having no fons of all his race remaining a-
live, and only this to maintain him on
his throne; and looking on this as a man
difobliged, firft by the rape of his miftrefs.
or 1ather wife and now by depriving
him wholly of her, he feared might
make him defperate, and do fome ciuel
thing, either to himfelf or his old grandfather the offender, he began to repent
him extremely of the contempt he had,
in his rage, put on Imoinda. Befides,
he confidered, he ought in honour to have
killed her for this offence, if it had been
one. He ought to have had fo much value and confideration for a maid of her
quality, as to have nobly put her to death
and not to have fold her like a common
flave; the greateft revenge and moft dif-
graceful of any, and to which they pre-
fer death, a thoufand times and implore

it;

it ; as Imoinda did, but coul
that honour. Seeing ther
certain that Oroonoko whould mighy re
fent this affront, he thought good to make
fome excufe for his rafhnefs to him ; and
to that end, he fent a meffenger to the
camp, with orders to treat with him a-
bout the matter, to gain his pardon, and
endeavour to mitigate his grief: but that
by no means he fhould tell him fhe was
fold, but fecretly put to death; for he
knew he fhould never obtain his pardon
for the other.

When the meffenger came, he found
the prince upon the point of engaging
with the enemy; but as foon as he heard
of the arrival of the meffenger, he commanded him to his tent, where he em-
braced him, and received him with joy;
which was foon abated by the down-caft
looks of the meffenges, who was inftant-
ly demanded the caufe by Oroonoko ;
who, impatient of delay, afked a thouf-
and queftions in a breath and all concerning Imoinda. But their needed little return; for he could almoft anfwer himfelf of all he demanded, from his fight and
eyes.

t the meffenger cafting him-,
inces's feet, and kiffing them,
e fubmiffion of a man that had
fomething to implore which he dreaded
to utter, befought him to hear with calm-
nefs what he had to deliver to him, and
to call up all his noble and heroic courage, to encounter with his words, and
defend himfelf againft the ungrateful
things he had to relate. Oroonoko replied with a deep figh, and a languifhing
voice,—I am armed againft their worft
efforts—For I know they will tell me
Imoinda is no more—And after that you
may fpare the reft. Then commanding
him to rife, he laid himfelf on a carpet,
under a rich pavilion, and remained a
good while filent, and was hardly heard
to figh. When he was come a little to
himfelf, the meffenger afked him leave
to deliver that part of his embaffy which
the prince had not yet divined : And the
prince cry'd, I permit thee—Then he
told him the affliction the king was in,
for the rafhnefs he had committed in
cruelty to Imoinda, and how he deigned
to afk pardon for his offence, and to im-

plore

plore the prince would not
lofs to touch his heart too fen,
now all the gods could not reftore man,
but might recompence him in glory,
which he begged he would purfue; and
that death, that common revenger of all
injuries, will foon even the account between him and a feeble old man.

Oroonoko bad him return his duty to
his lord and mafter, and to affure him,
there was no account of revenge to be ad-
jufted between them if there was, he
was the aggreffor, and that death would
be juft, and, mauger his age, would fee
him righted; and he was contented to
leave his fhare of glory to youths more
fortunate and worthy of that favour
from the gods: that henceforth he would
never lift a weapon or draw a bow, but
abandon the fmall remains of his life
to fighs and tears and the continual
thoughts of what his lord and grandfather
had thought good to fend out of the
world, with all that youth, that innocence and beauty.

After

ng spoken this, whatever his
.ers and men of the best rank
coul , they could not raise him from
the carpet, or persuade him to action,
and resolutions of life; but commanding
all to retire, he shut himself into his pa-
villion all that day, while the enemy
was ready to engage; and wond'ring at
the delay, the whole body of the chief
of the army then addressed themselves to
to him, and to whom they had much ado
to get admittance. They fell on their
faces at the foot of his carpet, where
they lay, and besought him with earnest
prayers and tears to lead them forth to
battle, and not let the enemy take advantages of them; and implored him to
have regard to his glory, and to the world
that depended on his courage and conduct. But he made no other reply to
all their supplications than this, That he
had now no more business for glory;
and for the world it was a trifle not worth
his care: 'Go, (continued he, sighing)
and divide it amongst you, and reap with
joy what you so vainly prize, and leave
me to my more welcome destiny.'

They

They then demanded wi.
do, and whom he would cc
room, that the confusion o
youth and power might not ruin then
order, and make them a prey to their
enemies. He replied, he would not give
himself that trouble—but wished them to
chuse the bravest man among't them, let
his quality or birth be what it would.
' For, oh my friends, (says he) it is not
titles make men brave or good ; or birth
that bestows courage and generosity, or
makes the owner happy. Believe this
when you behold Oroonoko the most
wretched, and abandoned by fortune, or
all the creation of the gods ' So turning himself about, he would make no
more reply to all they could urge or
implore.

The army beholding their officers return unsuccessful, with sad faces and om-
nious looks, that presaged no good luck,
suffered a thousand fears to take possesi-
sion of their hearts, and the enemy to
come even upon them before they could
provide for their safety by any defence
and tho' they were assured by some who

had

had a mind to animate them, that they should be immediately headed by the prince; and that in the mean time Aboan had orders to command as general; yet they were so dismay'd for want of that great example of bravery, that they could make but a very feeble resistance; and, at last, downright fled before the enemy who pursued them to the very tents, killing them: nor could all Aboan's courage which that day gained him immortal glory, shame 'em into a manly defence of themselves. The guards that were left behind about the prince's tent, seeing the soldiers flee before the enemy, and scatter themselves all over the plain, in great disorder, made such out-cries as rouzed the prince from his am'rous slumber, in which he had remained buried for two days, without permitting any sustenance to approach him. But, in spite of all his resolutions, he had not the constancy of grief to that degree, as to make him insensible of the danger of his army; and in that instant he leaped from his couch, and cry'd—'Come if we must die, let us
' meet death the noblest way; and 'twill

'be

' be more like Oroonoko to encounter
' him at an army's head, oppofing the
' torrent of a conquering foe, than lazi-
' ly on a couch to wait his lingering
' pleafure, and die every moment by a
' thoufand racking thoughts ; or be tame-
' ly taken by an enemy, and led a whin-
' ing, love-fick flave to adorn the tri-
' umphs of Jamoan that young victor,
' who already is entered beyond the li-
' mits I have prefcribed him '

While he was fpeaking, he fuffered his
people to drefs him for the field ; and
fallying out of his pavilion, with more
life and vigour in his countenance than
ever he fhewed he appeared like fome
divine power defcended to fave his country from deftruction· and his people had
purpofely put him on all things that might
make him fhine with moft fplendor, to
ftrike a reverend awe into the beholders.
He flew into the thickeft of thofe that
were purfuing his men ; and being ani-
mated with defpair, he fought as if he
came on purpofe to die, and did fuch
things as will not be believed that human
ftrength could perform ; and fuch as

foon

soon inspired all the rest with new courage, and new ardour. And now it was that they began to fight indeed; and so as if they would not be out-done even by their adored hero; who turning the tide of the victory, changing absolutely the fate of the day, gained an entire conquest: And Oroonoko having the good fortune to single out Jamoan, he took him prisoner with his own hand, having wounded him almost to death.

This Jamoan afterwards became very dear to him, being a man very gallant, and of excellent graces, and fine parts; so that he never put him amongst the rank of captives as they used to do, without distinction, for the common sale, or market, but kept him in his own court, where he retained nothing of the prisoner but the name, and returned no more into his own country; so great an affection he took for Oroonoko, and by a thousand tales and adventures of love and gallantry, flattered his disease of melancholly and languishment; which I have often heard him say, had certainly killed him, but for the conversation of this prince &

A hout

Aboan, and the French governor he had from his childhood, of whom I had spoken before, and who was a man of admirable wit, great ingenuity and learning; all which he had infused into his young pupil. This Frenchman was banished out of his own country, for some heretical notions he held; and tho' he was a man of very little religion, yet he had admirable morals, and a brave soul.

After the total defeat of Jamoan's army, which all fled, or were left dead upon the place, they spent some time in the camp; Oroonoko choosing rather to remain a while there in his tents than to enter into a palace, or live in a court where he had so lately suffered so great a loss. The officers therefore, who saw and knew his cause of discontent, invented all forts of diversions and sports to entertain their prince : so that what with those amusements abroad, and others at home, that is, within their tents, with the persuasions, arguments, and care of his friends and servants that he more peculiarly prized, he wore off in time a great part of that chagrin, and torture of

despair

defpair, which the firft efforts of Imoinda's death had given him; infomuch as having received a thoufand kind embaffies nom the king, and invitations to return to court, he obeyed, tho' with no little reluctancy; and when he did fo, there was a vifible change in him, and for a long time he was much more melancholy than before. But time leffens all extremes, and reduces them to mediums, and unconcein; but no motives of beauties, tho' all endeavoured it, could engage him in any fort of amour, tho' he had all the invitations to it, both from his own youth and other ambitions and defigns.

Oroonoko was no fooner returned from this laft conqueft, and received at court with all the joy and magnificence that could be expreffed to a young victor, who was not only returned triumphant, but beloved like a deity, than there arrived in port an Englifh veffel.

The mafter of it had often before been in thefe countries, and was very well known to Oroonoko, with whom he had
trafficked

trafficked for flaves, and had ufed to do
the fame with his predeceffors.

This commander was a man of a finer
fort of addrefs and converfation, better
bred, and more engaging, than moft of
that fort of men are ; fo that he feemed
rather never to have been bred out of a
court, than almoft all his life at fea —
This captain therefore was always better received at court, than moft of the
traders to thofe countries were ; and efpecially by Oroonoko, who was more
civilized, according to the European
mode, than any other had been, and took
more delight in the white nations ; and,
above all men of parts and wit. To this
captain he fold abundance of his flaves,
and for the favour and efteem he had for
him, made him many prefents. and o-
bliged him to ftay at court as long as
poffibly he could. Which the captain
feemed to take as a very great honour
done him, entertaining the prince every
day with globes and maps, and mathema-
tical difcourfes and inftruments ; eating,
drinking, hunting, and living with him
with fo much familiarity, that it was not

to

to be doubted but he had gained very greatly upon the heart of this gallant young man. And the captain in return for all thefe mighty favours, befought the prince to honour his veffel with his pre- ience fome day or other at dinner, befo1e he fhould fet fail ; which he condefcend- ed to accept, and appointed his day. — The captain on his part, failed not to have all things in a readinefs, in the moft magnificent o1der he could poffibly, and the day being come, the captain in his boat, richly adorned with carpets and velvet cufhions, rowed to the fhore, to receive the prince ; with another long- boat, where was placed all his mufic and trumpets, with which Oroonoko was extremely delighted ; who met him on the fhore, attended by his French go- vernor, Jamoan, Aboan, and about an hundred of the nobleft youths of the court: and after they had firft carried the prince on board, the boats fetched the reft off; where they found a very fplendid treat, with all forts of fine wines ; and were as well entertained, as 'twas poffible in fuch a place to be.

The

The prince having drank hard of punch
and feveral forts of wine, as did all the
reft, (for great care was taken they fhould
want nothing of that part of the entertainment) was very merry, and in great
admiration of the fhip, for he had never
been in one before ; fo that he was curious in beholding every place where he
decently might defcend. The reft no lefs
curious, who were not quite overcome
with drinking, rambled at their pleafure
fore and aft, as their fancies guided 'em:
fo that the captain, who had well laid
his defign before, gave the word, and
feized on all his guefts : they clapping
great irons fuddenly on the prince, when
he was leaped down into the hold. to view
that part of the veffel, and locking him
faft down, fecured him. The fame treat-
chery was ufed to all the reft, and all
in one inftant, in feveral places of the
fhip, were lafhed faft in irons, and betrayed to flavery. That great defign over
they fet all hands at work to hoift fail,
and with as treacherous as fair a wind
they made from the fhore with this innocent

cent and glorious prize. who thought of
nothing less than such an entertainment.

Some have commended this act as brave
n the captain ; but I will spare my sense
of it, and leave it to my reader to judge
as he pleases. It may be easily guessed
in what manner the prince resented this
indignity, who may be best resembled
to a lion taken in a toil ; so he raged,
so he struggled for liberty but all in vain.
and they had so wisely managed his fetters, that he could not use a hand in his
defence, to quit himself of a life that
would by no means endure slavery ; nor
could he move from the place where he
was tied, to any solid part of the ship,
against which he might have beat his head
and have finished his disgrace that way.
So that being deprived of all other means
he resolved to perish for want of food ;
and pleased at last with that thought and
toiled and tired by rage and indignation,
he laid himself down, and sullenly resolved upon dying, and refused all things
that were brought him.

This

This did not a little vex the captain, and more so as he found almost all of them of the same humour; so that the loss of so many brave slaves, so tall and goodly to behold, would have been very considerable; he therefore ordered one of his men to go from him (for he would not be seen himself) to Oroonoko, and to assure him, he was afflicted for having rashly done so unhospitable a deed, and which could not be now remedied, since they were so far from shore; but since he resented it in so high a nature, he assured him he would revoke his resolution, and set both him and his friends ashore on the next land they touched at, and of this the messenger gave him his oath, provided he would resolve to live. And Oroonoko, whose honour was such as he never had violated a word in his life himself, much less a solemn asseveration, believed in an instant what this man said, but replied, he expected for a confirmation of this, to have his shameful fetters dismissed. This demand was carried to the captain; who returned him answer, that the offence had been so

great

-eat which he had put upon the prince, that he durſt not truſt him with liberty while he remained in the ſhip, for fear, left by a valour natural to him, and a revenge that would animate that valour, he might commit ſome outrage fatal to himſelf, and the king his maſter to whom the veſſel did belong. To this Oroono-ko replied, he would engage his honour to behave himſelf in all friendly order and manner, and obey the command of the captain, as he was lord of the king's veſſel, and general of thoſe men under his command.

This was delivered to the ſtill doubt-ing captain, who could not reſolve to truſt a heathen, he ſaid, upon his parole, a man that had no ſenſe or notion of the god that he worſhipped. Oroonoko then replied, he was very ſorry to hear that the captain pretended to the knowledge and worſhip of any Gods, who had taught um no better principles, than not to credit as he would be credited; but they told him the difference of their faith oc-caſioned that diſtruſt; for the captain had proteſted to him upon the word of

a chriftian, and fworn in the name of
a great God ; which if he fhould violate
he muft expect eteinal torments in the
world to come. 'Is that all the obliga-
' he has to be juft to his oath ? (reply'd
' Oroonoko) let him know, I fwear by
' my honour; which to violate, would
' not only render me cortemptible and
' defpifed by all brave and honeft men,
' and fo give myfelf perpetual pain, but
' it would be eternally offending and dif-
' pleafing all mankind ; harming betray-
' ing, circumventing, and outraging all
' men. But punifhments hereafter are
' fuffered by one's felf; and the world
' takes no cognizance whether this God
' has revenged them or not, 'tis done fo
' fecretly, and deferr'd fo long ; while
' the man of no honour fuffers every
' moment the fcorn and contempt of the
' honefter world, and dies every day ig-
' nominioufly in his fame, which is
' more valuable than life. I fpeak not
' this to move belief, but to fhew you
' miftake when you imagine, that he
' who would violate his honour, will
' keep his word with his gods.' So tuin-
ing

g from him with a difdainful fmile, he
fufed to anfwer him, when he urged
him to know what anfwer he fhould carry
back to his captain; fo that he departed
without faying any more.

The captain pondering and confulting
what to do, it was concluded that nothing but Oroonoko's liberty would encourage any of the reft to eat, except
the Frenchman, whom the captain could
not pretend to keep prifoner, but only
told him he was fecured becaufe he might
act fomething in favour of the prince;
but that he fhould be freed as foon as he
came to land. So that he concluded it
wholly neceffary to free the prince from
his irons, that he might fhew himfelf to
the reft; that they might have an eye
upon him, and that they could not fear a
fingle man.

This being refolved, to make the ob-
ligation the greater, the captain himfelf
went to Oroonoko; where, after many
compliments, and affurances of what he
had already promifed, he receiving from
the prince his parole, and his hand, for
his good behaviour, difmiffed his irons,
and

and brought him to his own cabin ; where
after having treated and reposed him a
while, (for he had neither eat nor slept
for four days before) he besought him
to visit those obstinate people in chains,
who refused all manner of sustenance ;
and intreated him to oblige them to eat,
and assure them of their liberty the first
opportunity.

Oroonoko, who was too generous not
to give credit to his words, shewed himself to his people, who were transported
with excess of joy at the sight of their
darling prince ; falling at his feet, and
kissing and embracing them ; believing,
as some divine oracle, all he assured 'em.
But he besought them to bear their chains
with that bravery that became those whom
he had seen act so nobly in arms ; and
that they could not give him greater
proofs of their love and friendship,
since it was all the security the captain
(his friend) could have against the revenge, he said, they might possibly justly
take for the injuries sustained by him.
And they all, with one accord, assured
him

him, that they could not suffer enough, when it was for his repose and safety.

After this, they no longer refused to eat, but took what was brought them, and were pleased with their captivity, since by it they hoped to redeem the prince, who, all the rest of the voyage, was treated with all the respect due to his birth, tho' nothing could divert his melancholly ; and he would often sigh for Imoinda, and think this a punishment due to his misfortunes, in having left that noble maid behind him, that fatal night in the Otan, when he fled to the camp.

Possessed with a thousand thoughts of past joys with this fair young person, and a thousand griefs for her eternal loss, he endured a tedious voyage, and at last arrived at the mouth of the river of Surinam, a colony belonging to the King of England, and where they were to deliver some part of their slaves. There the merchants and gentlemen of the country going on board, to demand those lots of slaves they had alredy agreed on ; and, amongst those, the overseers of those plantations where I then chanc'd to be.

The

The captain, who had given the word,
order'd his men to bring up those noble
slaves in fetters whom I have spoken of,
and having put 'em, some in one and
some in other lots with women and children, (which they call Pickaninies) they
sold them off as slaves, to several merchants and gentlemen ; not putting any
two in one lot, because they would
separate 'em far from each other ; nor
daring to trust 'em upon contriving some
great action, to the ruin of the colony.

Oroonoko was first seiz'd on, and sold
to our overseer, who had the first lot,
with seventeen more of all sorts and sizes,
but not one of quality with him. When
he saw this, he found what they meant;
for, as I said, he understood English pretty
well ; and being wholly unarm'd and de-
fenceless, so as it was in vain to make any
resistance he only beheld the captain with
a look all fierce and disdained, upbraiding
him with eyes that forc'd blushes on his
guilty cheeks, and cry'd in passing over
the side of the ship ; 'Farewel, Sir, tis
worth my sufferings to gain so true a
konwledge, both of you, and of your gods
by

by whom you fwear. And defiring thofe
that held him to forbear their pains, and
telling 'em he would make no refiftance,
he cry'd ' Come, my fellow-flaves, let
us defcend, and fee if we can meet with
more honour and honefty in the next
world we fhall touch upon. So he nimbly
leapt into the boat, and fhewing no more
concern, fuffer'd himfelf to be row'd up
the river, with his feventeen compa-
nions.

The gentleman that bought him, was
a young Cornifh gentleman, whofe name
was Trefry, a man of great wit, and
fine learning, and was carried into thofe
parts by the Lord ——, Governor, to
manage all his affairs. He reflecting on
the laft words of Oroonoko to the captain, and beholding the richnefs of his
veft, no fooner came into the boat, but
he fixed his eyes on him, and finding
fomething fo extraordinary in his face,
his fhape and his mien, a greatnefs of
look, and haughtinefs in his air, and finding he fpoke Englifh, had a great mind to
be enquiring into his quality and fortune;
which, though Oroonoko endeavoured to

hide

hide, by only confeſſing he was above
the rank of common ſlaves, Trefry ſoon
found he was yet ſomething greater than
he confeſſed; and from that moment began to conceive ſo vaſt an eſteem for him
that he ever after loved him as his deareſt
brother, and ſhewed him all the civili-
ties due to ſo great a man.

Trefry was a very good mathemati-
cian, and a linguiſt; could ſpeak French
and Spaniſh, and in the three days they
remained in the boat, (for ſo long were
they going from the ſhip to the plantation) he entertained Oroonoko ſo agree-
ably with his art and diſcourſe, that he
was no leſs pleaſed with Trefry, than
he was with the prince; and he thought
himſelf, at leaſt, fortunate in this, that
ſince he was a ſlave, as long as he could
ſuffer himſelf to remain ſo, he had a man
of ſo excellent wit and parts for a maſter. So that before they had finiſhed
their voyage up the river, he made no
ſcruple of declaring to Trefry all his
fortunes, and moſt part of what I have
here related, and put himſelf wholly in
to the hands of his new friend, who he
                                    found

found refented all the injuries done him, and was charmed with all the greatneffes of his actions, which were recited with that modefty, and delicate fenfe, as wholly vanquifhed him, and fubdued him to his intereft. And he promifed him, on his word and honour. he would find the means to re-conduct him to his own country again; affuring him he had a perfect abhorrence of fo difhonourable an action; and that he would fooner have died. than have been the author of fuch a perfidy. He found the prince was very much concerned to know what became of his friends, and how they took their flavery; and Trefry promifed to take care about the enquiring after their condition, and that he fhould have an account of them.

Tho' as Oroonoko afterwards faid, he had little reafon to credit the words of a Backearary; yet he knew not why, but he faw a kind of fincerity, and awful truth in the face of Trefry; he faw honefty in his eyes, and he found him wife and witty enough to underftand honour·

for

for it was one of his maxims, A man of wit could not be a knave or villain.

In their paſſage up the river, they put in at ſeveral houſes for refreſhment; and even when they landed, numbers of people would flock to behold this man · not but their eyes were daily entertained with the ſight of ſlaves; but the fame of Oroonoko was gone before him, and all people were in admiration of his beauty.— Beſides he had a rich habit on, in which he was taken, ſo different from the reſt, and which the captain could not ſtrip him of becauſe he was forced to ſurprize his perſon in the minute he ſold him. When he found his habit made him liable as he thought, to be gazed at the more, he begged of Trefry to give him ſomething more befitting a ſlave, which he did, and took off his robes : nevertheleſs he ſhone through all, and his Oſenbrigs (a ſort of brown Holland ſuit he had on) could not conceal the graces of his looks and mien ; and he had no leſs admirers than when he had his dazling habit on. the royal youth appeared in ſpite of the ſlave, and people could not help treating him after a different manner without designing it. As soon as they approached him they venerated and esteemed him; his eyes insensibly commanded respect, and his behaviour insinuated it into every soul. So that there was nothing talked of but this young and gallant slave, even by those who yet knew not that he was a prince.

I ought to tell you, that the christians never buy any slaves but they give them some name of their own, their native ones being likely very barbarous and hard to pronounce; so that Mr. Trefry gave Oroonoko that of Cæsar · which name will live in that Country as long as that (scarce more) glorious one of the great Roman · for 'tis most evident he wanted no part of the personal courage of that Cæsar, and acted things as memorable, had they been done in some part of the world replenished with people and historians, that might have given him his due. But his misfortune was, to fall into an obscure world, that afforded only a female pen to celebrate his fame, tho' I doubt not but it had lived from others

endeavours

endeavours, if the Dutch, who immediately after his time took that country,
had not killed, banished, and dispersed
all those that were capable of giving the
world this great man's life. much better
than I have done And Mr Trefry, who
designed it, died before he began it, and
bemoaned himself for not having under-
took it in time.

For the future therefore I must call O-
roonoko, Cæsar ; since by that name only
he was known in our western world, and
by that name he was received on shore
at Parham-house, where he was destined
a slave. But if the king himself (God
bless him) had come on shore, there could
not have been greater expectations by all
the whole plantation, and those neighbouring ones, than was on ours at that
time , and he was received more like a
governor then a slave : notwithstanding
as the custom was, they assigned him his
portion of land, his house and his business up in the plantations. But as it was
more for form than any design to put him
to his task, he endured no more of the
slave but the name, and remained some

days

in the houfe, receiving all vifits that were made him, without ftirring towards that part of the plantation where the negroes were.

At laft, he needs would go view his land, his houfe, and the bufinefs affigned him. But he no fooner came to the houfes of the flaves, which are like a little town by itfelf, the negroes having all left work but they all came forth to behold him, and fo nd he was that prince who had at feveral times, fold moft of them to thefe parts; and from a veneration they pay to great men, efpecially if they know them, and from the furprize and awe they had at the fight of him, they all caft themfelves at his feet, and crying out, in their language. Live, O king! Long live, O king! and kiffing his feet, paid him even divine homage.

Several Englifh gentlemen were with him, and what Mr. Trefry had told 'em was here confirm'd. of which he himfelf before had no other witnefs than Cæfar, himfelf; But he was infinitely glad to find his grandeur confirmed by the adoration of all the flaves.

C 4 Cæfar

Cæfar, troubled with their over-joy, and overceremony, befought 'em to rife, and to receive him as their fellow-flave affuring them he was no better. At which they fet up with one accord a moft terrible and hideous mourning and condoling, which he and the Englifh had much ado to appeafe but at laft they prevail'd with them, and they prepar'd all their barbarous mufick, and every one kill'd and drefs'd fomething of his own flock [for every family has their land apart, on which, at their leifure-times, they breed all eatable things] and clubbing it together, made a moft magnificent fupper inviting their grandee captain their prince to honour t with his prefence, which he did and feveral Englifh with him, where they all waited on him, fome playing, others dancing before him all the time, according to the manners of their feveral nations, and with unwearied induftry endeavouring to pleafe and delight him.

While they fet at meat, Mr. Trefry told Cæfar, that moft of thefe young flaves were undone in love with a fine fhe flave, whom they had had about fix months on

their

their land. The prince, who never heard the name of love without a figh, nor any mention of it without the curiosity of examining further into that tale, which of all discourses was most agreeable to him, asked how they came to be so unhappy, as to be all undone for one fair slave? Trefry, who was naturally amorous and delighted to talk of love as well as any body, proceeded to tell him, they had the most charming Black that ever was beheld on their plantation, about fifteen or sixteen years old, as he guess'd, that for his part he had done nothing but figh for her ever since she came; and that all the white beauties he had seen, never charm'd him so absolutely as this fine creature had done; and that no man, of any nation, ever beheld her, that did not fall in love with her; and that she had all the slaves perpetually at her feet; and the whole country resounded with the fame of Clemene, for so (said he) we have christen'd her · but she denies us all with such a noble disdain, that 'tis a miracle to see, that she who can give such eternal desire, should herself be all ice:

C 5   and

and all unconcern. She is adorn'd with
the most graceful modesty that ever beau-
tify'd youth ; the softest sigher-----that,
if she were capable of love, one would
swear she languish'd for some absent
happy man; and so retired, as if she fear'd
a rape even from the God of day, or that
the breeze would steal kisses from her,
delicate mouth. Her task of work some
sighing lover every day makes it his peti-
tion to perform for her; which she accepts
blushing, and with reluctancy, for fear
he will ask her a look for a recompence,
which he dares not perfume to hope ; so
great an awe she strikes into the hearts
of her admirers. ' I do not wonder (re-
' ply'd the prince) that Clemene should
' refuse slaves, being, as you say, so
' beautiful, but wonder how she escapes
' those that can entertain her as you can
' do ; or why, being your slave, you do
' not oblige her to yield? I confess (said
' Trefry) when I have against her will,
' entertained her with love so long, as to
' be transported with my passion even
' above decency, I have been ready to
' make use of those advantages of strength

'and force nature has given me; But
'Oh! she disarms me with that modesty,
'and weeping, so tender and so moving,
'that I retire, and thank my stars she
'overcame me' The company laugh'd
at his civility to a slave, and Cæsar only applauded the nobleness of his passion and nature, since that slave might be
noble, or what was better, have true notions of honour and virtue in her. Thus
passed they this night after having received from the slaves all imaginable respect and obedience.

The next day, Trefry asked Cæsar to
walk when the heat was allayed, and de-
signedly carried him by the cottage of the
fair slave; and told him, she whom he
spoke of last night lived there retired.
But (says he) I would not wish you to
approach; for I am sure you will be in
love as soon as you behold her. Cæsar
assured him, he was proof against all the
charms of that sex; and that if he imagined his heart could be so perfidious to
love again after Imoinda, he believed hi
would tear it from his bosom. They had
no sooner spoke, but a little shock-dog
that

that had been given Clemene, which
she took great delight in, ran out; and
she, not knowing any body was there,
run to get it in again, and bolted out on
those who were just speaking of her
When seeing them she would have run in
again, but Trefry caught her by the hand
and cry'd Clemene, however you fly a
lover, you ought to pay some respect to
this stranger, (pointing to Cæsar). But
she, as if she had resolved never to raise
her eyes to the face of a man again, bent
them the more to the earth when he spoke
and gave the prince the leisure to look
the more at her. There needed no long
gazing, or consideration, to examine who
this fair creature was; he soon saw Imoinda all over her, in a minute he saw her
face, her shape, her air, her modesty, and
all that called forth his soul with joy at
his eyes, and left his body almost desti-
tute of life; it stood without motion, and
for a minute knew not that it had a being; and, I believe, he had never come
to himself, so oppressed he was with over-
joy, if he had not met with this allay,
that he perceived Imoinda fall dead in the
hands

hands of Trefry. This awakened him, and he ran to her aid, and caught her in his arms, where by degrees she came to herself; and 'tis needless to tell with what transports, what extasies of joy, they both a while beheld each other, without speaking; then snatched each other to their arms; then gaze again as if they still doubted whether they possessed the blessing they grasped: but when they recovered their speech, 'tis not to be imagined what tender things they expressed to each other; wondering what strange fate had brought them again together. They soon inform'd each other of their fortunes and equally bewailed their fate, but at the same time they protested, that even fetters and slavery were soft and easy, and would be supported with joy and pleasure, while they could be so happy to possess each other, and to be able to make good their vows. Cæsar swore he disdained the empire of the world, while he could behold his Imoinda; and she despised grandeur and pomp, those vanities of her sex, when she could gaze on O-roonoko. He adored the very cottage

C 7   where

where she resided, and said, that little inch of the world would give him more happiness than all the universe could do; and she vowed it was a palace, while adorend with the presence of Oroonoko.

Trefry was infinitely pleased with this novel, and found this Clemene was the fair mistress of whom Cæsar had before spoke; and was not a little satisfied, that heaven was so kind to the prince as to sweeten his misfortunes by so lucky an accident; and leaving the lovers to themselves, was impatient to come down to Parham-house (which was on the same plantation, to give me an account of what had happened. I was as impatient to make their lovers a visit having already made a friendship with Cæsar, and from his own mouth learned what I have related; which was confirmed by his Frenchman, who was set on shore to seek his fortune and of whom they could not make a slave, because a christian : and he came daily to Parham-hill to see and pay his respects to his pupil prince. So that concerning and interesting myself in all that related to Cæsar, whom I had assured of

liberty

liberty as foon as the governor arrived, I
hafted prefently to the place where thefe
lovers were, and was infinitely glad to
find this beautiful young flave [who had
already gained all our efteems, for her
modefty and extraordinary prettinefs] to
be the fame I had heard Cæfar fpeak fo
much of One may imagine then we paid
her a treble refpect ; and tho' from her
being carved in fine flowers and birds o-
ver her body, we took her to be of quality before, yet when we knew Clemene
was Imoinda, we could not enough ad-
mire her.

I had forgot to tell you, that thofe who
are nobly born of that country, are fo de-
licately cut and raifed all over the fore-
part of the trunk of their bodies, that it
looks as if they were japan'd, the works
being raifed like high point round the
edges of the flowers. Some are only
carved with a little flower or bird, at the
fides of the temples, as was Cæfar ; and
thofe who are fo carved over the body,
refemble our ancient Picts that are figur-
ed in the chronicles , but thefe carvings
are more delicate.

From

From that happy day Cæsar took Clemene for his wife, to the general joy of all people; and there was as much magnificence as the country cou'd afford at the celebration of the wedding. And in very short time after she conceived with child, which made Cæsar even adore her, knowing he was the last of his great race. This new incident made him more impatient of liberty, and he was every day treating with Trefry for his & Clemene's liberty, and offered either gold or a vast quantity of slaves, which should be paid before they let him go, provided he could have any security that he should go when his ranfom was paid. They fed him from day to day with promisses, and delay'd him till the lord governor should come; so that he began to suspect them of fulhood, and that they would delay him till the time of his wife's delivery and make a slave of the child too, for all the breed is theirs to whom the parents belong.— This thought made him very uneasy, and his sullenness gave them some jealousies of him; so that I was obliged, by some persons who feared a mutiny [which is

- very

very fatal sometimes in those colonies that abound so with slaves, that they exceed the whites in vast numbers] to discourse with Cæsar, and to give him all the satisfaction I possibly could. They knew that he and Clemene were scarce an hour in a day from my lodgings; that they eat with me, and that I obliged them in all things I was capable. I entertained them with the lives of the Romans and great men which charmed him to my company; and her, with teaching her all the pretty works that I was mistress of, and telling her stories of nuns, and endeavouring to bring her to the knowledge of the true God. But of all discourses, Cæsar liked that the worst, and would never be reconciled to our notions of the Trinity, of which he ever made a jest; it was a riddle he said would turn his brain to conceive, and one could not make him understand what faith was. — However these conversations failed not altogether so well to divert him, that he liked the company of us women much above the men, for he could not drink, and he is but an ill companion in that
country

country that cannot. So that obliging
him to love us very well, we had all the
liberty of speech with him, especially
myself, whom he called his great mistress ; and indeed my word would go a
great way with him. For these reasons
I had opportunity to take notice to him,
that he was not well pleased of late, as
he used to be : was more retired and
thoughtful ; and told him, I took it ill he
should suspect we would break our words
with him, and not permit both him and
Clemene to return to his own kingdom,
which was not so long away, but when he
was once on his voyage he would quickly
arrive there. He made me some answers
that shewed a doubt in him, which made
me ask what advantage it would be to
doubt? It would but give us a fear of
him, and possibly compel us to treat him
so as I should be very loth to behold ;
that is it might occasion his confinement.
Perhaps this was not so luckily spoke of
of me, for I perceived he resented that
word, which I strove to soften again in
vain. However he assured me, that what-
soever resolutions he should take, he
                                        would

would act nothing upon the white people ; and as for myself, and those upon
that plantation where he was, he would
sooner forfeit his eternal liberty, and life
itself, than lift his hand against his greatest
enemy on that place. He besought me
to suffer no fears upon his account, for
he could do nothing that honour shou'd not
dictate ; but he accused himself for having suffered slavery so long ; yet he charg-
ed that weakness on love alone, who was
capable of making him neglect even glory
itself ; and for which now he reproaches
himself every moment of the day. Much
more to this effect he spoke, with an air
impatient enough to make me know he
would not be long in bondage ; and tho'
he suffered only the name of a slave, and
had nothing of the toil and labour of one,
yet that was sufficient to render him uneasy ; and he had been too long idle, who
used always to be in action, and in arms.
He had a spirit all rough and fierce, and
that could not be tam'd to lazy rest: And
tho' all endeavours were used to exercise
himself in such actions and sports as this
would

world afforded, as running, wreſtling, pitching the bar, hunting and fiſhing, chaſing and killing tygers of a monſtrous ſize, which the continent affords in abundance ; and wonderful ſnakes, ſuch as Alexander is reported to have encountered at the river of Amazons, which Cæſar took great delight to overcome · yet theſe were not actions great enough for his large ſoul, which was ſtill panting after more renowned actions.

Before I parted that day with him, I got with much ado, a promiſe from him to reſt yet a little longer with patience, and wait the coming of the lord governor, who was every day expected on our ſhore. He aſſured me he would, and this promiſe he deſired me to know was given perfectly in complaiſance to me, in whom he had an entire confidence.

After this, I neither thought it convenient to truſt him much out of our view nor did the country who feared him ; but with one accord it was adviſed to treat him fairly, and oblige him to remain within ſuch a compaſs, and that he ſhould be permitted. as ſeldom as he could be, to go up to the plantations of the negroes, or, if he did, to be accompanied by some that should be rather, in appearance, attendants than spies. This care was for some time taken, and Cæsar looked upon it as a mark of extraordinary respect, and was glad his discontent had obliged them to be more observant to him. He received new assurances from the overseer which was confirmed to him, by all the gentlemen of the country, who made their court to him. During this time that we had his company more frequently than hitherto we had, it may not be unpleasant to relate to you the diversions we entertained him with, or rather he us.

My stay was to be short in that country because my father died at sea, and never arrived to possess the honour design'd him (which was lieutenant-general of six and thirty islands, besides the continent of Surinam), nor the advantages he hoped to reap by them: So that though we were obliged to continue on our voyage, we did not intend to stay upon the place. — Though, in a word, I must say thus much of it, that certainly had his late majesty,

of

of sacred memory, but seen and known what a vast and charming world he had been master of in that continent, he would never have parted so easily with it to the Dutch. 'Tis a continent whose vast extent was never yet known, and may contain more noble earth than all the universe beside ; for, they say it reaches from the east to the west one way as far as China, and another to Peru · It affords all things both for beauty and use ; 'tis there eternal spring, always the very months of April, May, and June ; the shades are perpetual, the trees bearing at once all degrees of leaves, and fruit, from blooming buds to ripe autumn · Groves of oranges, lemons, citrons, figs, nutmegs, and noble aromaticks, continually bearing their fragrancies ; the trees appearing all like nosegays, adorned with flowers of different kinds; some are all white some purple, some scarlet, some blue, some yellow ; bearing at the same time ripe fruit, and blooming young, or producing every day new. The very wood of these trees has an intrinsic value, above common timber; for they are when

cut

cut, of different colours, glorious to behold, and bear a price confiderable, to inlay withal. Befides this, they yield rich balm, and gums ; fo that we make our candles of fuch an aromatic fubftance as does not only give a fufficient light, but as they burn, they caft their perfumes all about. Cedar is the common firing, and all the houfes are built with it The very meat we eat, when fet on the table if it be native, I mean of the country, perfumes the whole room ; efpecially a little beaft called an Armadillo, a thing which I can liken to nothing fo well as a Rhinoceros ; 'tis all in white armour, fo jointed that it moves as well in it as if it had nothing on : This beaft is about the bignefs of a pig fix weeks old. But it were endlefs to give an account of all the divers wonderful and ftrange things that country affords, and which he took a great delight to go in fearch of; tho' thofe adventures are fometimes fatal, and at leaft dangerous. But while we had Cæfar in our company on thefe defigns, we feared no harm, nor fuffered any.

As foon as I came into the country the beft houfe in it was prefented me, call'd St. John's hill · It ftood on a vaft rock of white marble, at the foot of which, the river ran a vaft depth down, and not to be defcended on that fide ; the little waves ftill dafhing and wafhing the foot of this rock, made the fofteft murmurs and purlings in the world ; and the oppofite bank was adorned with fuch vaft quantities of different flowers eternally blowing, and every day and hour new, fenc'd behind them with lofty trees of a thoufand rare forms and colours that the profpect was the moft ravifhing that lands can create. On the edge of this white rock, towards the river, was a walk or grove, of orange and lemon trees, about half the length of the mall here, whofe flowry and fruit-bearing branches met at the top and hindered the fun, whofe rays are very fierce there, from entering a beam into the grove ; and the cool air that came from the river, made it not only fit to entertain people in, at all the hotteft hours of the day, but refrefh the fweet bloffoms, and made it always fweet and

charming;

charming; and sure the whole globe of
the world cannot shew so delightful a
place as this grove was: not all the gar-
dens of boasted Italy can produce a shade
to outvie this, which nature had joined
with art to render so exceeding fine; and
'tis a marvel to see how such vast trees
as big as English oaks, could take footing
on so solid a rock, and in so little earth
as covered that rock: But all things by
nature there are rare, delightful, & won
derful.   But to our sports

Sometimes we would go surprising,
and in search of young tygers in their dens
watching when the old ones went forth
to forage for prey; sometimes we have
been in great danger, and have fled apace
for our lives, when surprized by the dams.
But once above all other times, we went
on this design, and Cæsar was with us;
who had no sooner stolen a young tyger
from her nest, but going off we encountered the dam, bearing a buttock of a cow
which she had torn off with her mighty
paw, and going with it towards her den:
We had only four women, Cæsar and an
English gentleman, brother to Henry Martin,

tin the great Oliverian ; we found there was no escaping this enraged and ravenous beast. However we women fled as fast as we could from it ; but our heels had not faved our lives, if Cæfar had not laid down her cub, when he found the Tyger quit her prey to make the more speed towards him ; and taking Mr. Martin's fword, defired him to 'tand afide, or follow the ladies. He obeyed him ; and Cæfaa met this monftrous beast of mighty fize, and vast limbs, who came with open jaws upon him ; and fixing his awful ftern eyes full upon thofe of the beaft & putting himfelf into a very fteady and good aiming pofture of defence, ran his fword quite through her breaft, down to her very heart, home to the very hilt of the fword. The dying beaft ftretched out her paw, and going to grafp his thigh, furprized with death in that very moment did him no other harm than fixing her long nails in his flefh very deep, feebly wounded him, but could not grafp the life car of any. When he had done follow'd to us to return ; which re affurance of his victory, we

did, and found him lugging out the
fword from the bofom of the tyger, who
was laid in her blood on the ground.—
He took up the cub, and with an unconcern that had nothing of the joy or glad-
nefs of victory, he came and laid the
whelp at my feet. We all extremely
wonder'd at his daring, and at the bignefs
of the beaft, which was about the height
of an heifer, but of mighty great and
ftrong limbs.

Another time, being in the woods, he
killed a tyger, that had long infefted that
part, and born away abundance of fheep
and oxen, and other things that were for
the fupport of thofe to whom they belonged. Abundance of people affailed this
beaft, fome affirming they had fhot her
with feveral bullets quite through the
very heart; and they believed fhe was
a devil, rather than a mortal thing Cæfar had often faid, he had a mind to encounter this monfter, and fpoke with feveral gentlemen who had attempted her ;
one crying, I fhot her with fo many poi-
foned arrows, another with his gun in this
part of her, and another in that, fo that

ne remarking all the places where she was shot, fancied still he should overcome her by giving her another sort of a wound than any had yet done; and one day said [at the table] 'What trophies and gar-
' lands, ladies, will you make me, if I
' bring you home the heart of this raven-
' ous beast, that eats up all your lambs and pigs?' We all promised he should be rewarded at our hands. So taking a bow which he chose out of a great many, he went up into the wood, with two gentle-men where he imagined this devourer to be. They had not passed very far into it but they heared her voice, growling and grumbling, as if she was pleased with something she was doing. When they came in view, they found her muzzling in the belly of a new ravished sheep, which she had torn open; and seeing herself ap-proached. she took fast hold of her prey with her fore paws, and set a very fierce raging look on Cæsar, without offering to approach him, for fear at the same time of loosing what she had in possession: so that Cæsar remained a good while, only taking aim, and getting an opportunity

to shoot her where he designed. 'Twas
some time before he could accomplish it;
and to wound her, and not kill her, would
but have enraged her the more, and en-
dangered him. He had a quiver of arrows at his side, so that if one failed, he
could be supplied : At last, retiring a little, he gave her opportunity to eat, for he
found she was ravenous, and fell to as
soon as she saw him retire, being more
eager of her prey, than of doing new
mischiefs ; when he going softly to one
side of her, and hiding his person behind
certain herbage, that grew high and thick
he took so good an aim, that as he intended, he shot her just into the eye, and
the arrow was sent with so good a will,
and so sure a hand, that it stuck in her
brain, and made her caper and become
mad for a moment or two ; but being
seconded by another arrow, she fell dead
upon the prey. Cæsar cut her open with
a knife, to see where those wounds were
that had been reported to him, and why
she did not die of them. But I shall now
relate a thing, that, possibly will find no
credit among men ; because it is a notion
commonly

commonly received with us, that nothing can receive a wound in the heart and live . But when the heart of this courageous animal was taken out, there were feven bullets of lead in it. the wound feamed up with great fcars and fhe lived with the bullets a great while, for it was long fince they were fhot . this near the conqueror brought up to us, and 'twas a very great curiofity, which all the country came to fee ; and which gave Cæfar occafion of many fine difcourfes of accidents in war, and ftrange efcapes

At other times he would go a fifhing; and difcourfing on that diverfion. he found we had in that country a very ftrange fifh called a Numb-Eel, [an Eel of which I have eaten] that while it is alive. it has a quality fo cold, that thofe who are angling, though with a line of ever fo great a length with the rod at the end of it, it fhall in the fame minute the bait is touched by this Eel, feize him or her that holds the rod with a numbnefs, that fhall deprive him of fenfe for awhile; and fome have fallen into the water, and others dropped as dead on the banks of the ri-

ver

ver where they stood, as soon as this fish
touches the bait. Cæsar used to laugh at
this, and believed it impossible a man
could loose his force at the touch of a fish;
and could not understand that philosophy
that a cold quality should be of that nature; however he had a great curiosity
to try whether it would have the same
effect on him it had on others, and often
tried, but in vain. At last, the fought
for fish came to the bait, as he stood angling on the bank; and instead of throw-
ing away the rod, or giving it a sudden
twitch out of the water, whereby he
might have caught both the Eel and have
dismissed the rod, before it could have
too much power over him; for experi-
ments fake, he grasped it but the harder
and fainting fell into the river; and being still possessed of the rod, the tide
carried him, senseless as he was, a great
way, till an Indian Boat took him up;
and perceived when they touched him. a
numbness seize them, and by that knew
the rod was in his hand; which with a
paddle, (that is a short oar) they struck
away, and snatched it into the boat, eel
and

and all If Cæsar was almost dead, with
the effect of this fish, he was more so with
that of the water, where he had remained the space of going a league, and they
found they had much ado to bring him
back to life; but at last they did, and
brought him home, where he was in a
few hours well recovered and refreshed,
and not a little ashamed to find he should
be overcome by an eel, and that all the
people who heard his defiance, would
laugh at him. But we cheared him up;
and he being convinced, we had the eel
at supper, which was a quarter of an ell
about, and most delicate meat; and was
of the more value, since it cost so dear
as almost the life of so gallant a man.

About this time we were in many mortal fears, about some disputes the English had with the Indians; so that we could
scarce trust ourselves, without great numbers, to go to any Indian towns, or
place where they abode, for fear they
should fall upon us immediately after my
coming away; and the place being in the
possession of the Dutch, they used them
not so civilly as the English; so that they

cut

cut in pieces all they could take, getting into houfes, and hanging up the mother, and all her children about her ; and cut a footman I left behind me, all in joints, and nailed him to trees.

This feud began while I was there ; fo that I loft half the fatisfaction I propofed, not feeing and vifiting the Indian towns   But one day bemoaning of our misfortunes upon this account Cæfar told us, we need not fear, for if we had a mind to go, he would undertake to be our guard. Some would, but moft would not venture : About eighteen of us refolved, and took a barge ; and after eight days, arrived near an In lian town : But upon approaching it, the hearts of fome of our company failed, and they would not venture on fhore ; fo we polled, who would and who would not. For my part I faid, if Cæfar would, I would go.   He refolved, fo did my brother, and my woman a maid of good courage. Now none of us fpeaking the language of the people, and imagining we fhould have a half diverfion in gazing only ; and not knowing what they faid, we took a fifherman
that

that lived at the mouth of the river, who
had been a long inhabitant there, and o-
bliged him to go with us : But becaufe he
was known to the Indians, as trading a-
mong them, and being, by long living
there, become a perfect Indian in colour,
we, who had a mind to furprize them,
by making them fee fomething they never had feen, [that is, white people] refolved only myfelf, my brother and woman fhould go . So Cæfar, the fifherman,
and the reft, hiding behind fome thick
reeds and flowers that grew in the banks
let us pafs on towards the town, which
was on the banks of the river all along.
A little diftant from the houfes, or huts,
we faw fome dancing, others bufied in
fetching and carrying of water from the
river. They had no fooner efpied us,
but they fet up a loud cry, that frighten-
ed us at firft, we thought it had been for
thofe that fhould kill us, but it feems it
was of wonder and amazement. They
were all naked, and we were dreffed, fo
as is moft commode for the hot countries,
very glimmering and rich ; fo that we appeared extremely fine ; my own hair was

cut short, and I had a taffaty cap, with black feathers on my head; my brother was in a stuff suit, with silver loops and buttons, and abundance of green ribbon. This was all infinitely surprising to them and because we saw them stand still 'till we approached them, we took heart and advanced, came up to them and offered them our hands; which they took, and looked on us round about, calling still for more company; who came swarming out, all wondering, and crying out, Tepeeme: taking their hair up in their hands and spreading it wide to those they called out to; as if they would say, [as indeed it signified) Numberless Wonders, or not to be recounted, no more than to number the hair of their heads. By degrees they grew more bold, and from gazing upon us round, they touchled us, laying their hands upon all the features of our faces, feeling our breasts and arms, taking up one petticoat, than wondering to see another; admiring our shoes and stockings, but more our garters, which we gave them, and they ty'd about their legs, being lac'd with silver-lace at the

ends;

ends : for they much esteem any shining
things. In fine, we suffered them to sur-
vey us as they pleased, and we thought
they would never have done admiring us.
When Cæsar and the rest, saw we were
received with such wonder, they came up
to us; and finding the Indian traders whom
they knew, [for 'its by these fishermen,
called Indian traders, we hold a commerce
with them; for they love not to go far
from home, and we never go to them]
when they saw him therefore, they set up
a new joy, and cry'd in their language,
Oh, here's our Tiguamy, and we shall
know whether those things can speak —
So advancing to him, some of them gave
him their hands, and cry'd, Amora Tiguamy ; which is as much as, How do you
do ? Or, welcome, friend ; and all, with
one din, began to gabble to him, and ask'd
if we had sense and wit ? If we could talk
of affairs of life and war, as they could
do ? If we could hunt, swim, and do a thousand things they use ? He answer'd them
we could. Then they invited us into
their houses, and dress'd venison and buf-
falo for us · and going out, gather'd a lea

c

of a tree, called a Sarumbo leaf fix yards long, and fpread it on the ground for a table-cloth· and cutting another in pieces inftead of plates, fet us on little low Indian ftools, which they cut of one entire piece of wood, and paint in a fort of japan'd-work. They ferve every one their mefs on thefe pieces of leaves; and it was very good, but too high-feafon'd with pepper. When we had eat, my brother and I took out our flutes, and play'd 'em which gave 'em new wonder; and I foon perceived, by an admiration that is natural to thefe people, and by the extreme ignorance and fimplicity of 'em, it were not difficult to eftablifh any unknown or extravagant re-ligon among them, and to impofe any no-tions or fictions upon 'em. For feeing a kinfman of mine fet fome paper on fire with a burning-glafs, a trick they had never before feen, they were like to have adored him for a god, and begg'd he would give 'em the characters or figures of his name, that they might oppofe againft winds and ftorms; which he d. and they held it up in thofe feafons, a fancy'd it had a charm to conquer the

D

and kept it like a holy relic. They are very superstitious, and called him the great Peeie, that is Prophet. They shewed us their Indian Peeie, a youth about sixteen years old, as handsome as nature could make a man. They consecrate a beautiful youth from his infancy, and all arts are used to compleat him in the finest manner, both in beauty and shape. He is bred to all the little arts and cunning they are capable of: to all the Legerdemain tricks, and slight of hand, whereby he imposes on the rabble: and is both a Doctor in physic and divinity. And by these tricks make the sick believe he sometimes eases their pains, by drawing from the afflicted part little serpents, or odd flies, or worms, or any strange thing, and though they have besides undoubted good remedies for almost all their diseases, they cure the patient more by fancy than by medicines, and make them feared, loved, and reverenced. This young Peeie had a very young wife, who seeing my brother kiss her, came running and kissed me. After this they kissed one another, and made it a very great jest,

it

it being fo novel; and new admiration and laughing went round the multitude, that they never will forget that ceremony never before ufed or known. Cæfar had a mind to fee and talk with their war-captains, and we were conducted to one of their houfes, where we beheld feveral of their great captains, who had been at council But fo frightful a vifion it was to fee them, no fancy can create; no fad dreams can reprefent fo dreadful a fpectacle. For my part, I took them for hobgoblins, or fiends, rather than men. But however their fhapes appeared, their fouls were very humane and noble; but fome wanted their nofes. fome their lips, fome both nofes and lips, fome their ears, and others cut through each cheek, with long flafhes, through which their teeth appeared: They had feveral other formidable wounds and fcars, or rather difmembrings. They had comitia's or little fhort aprons before them, and girdles of cotton, with their knives naked ftuck in it; a bow at their back, and a quiver of arrows on their thighs; and moft had feathers on their heads of divers colours.

They

They cried, Amora Tiguamy to us, at our entrance, and were pleased we said the same to them; They seated us, and gave us drink of the best sort, and wondered as much as the others had done before, to see us Cæsar was marvelling as much at their faces, wondering how they should be so wounded in war; he was impatient to know how they all came by those frightful marks of rage or malice, rather than wounds got in noble battle · They told by our interpreter, that when any war was waging, two men chosen out by some old captain whose fighting was past, and who could only teach the theory of war, were to stand in competition for the generalship, or great war-captain; and being brought before the old judges, now past labour, they were asked, What they dare do, to shew they are worthy to lead an army? When he who is first asked, making no reply, cuts off his nose, and throws it contemptibly on the ground; and the other does something to himself which he thinks surpasses him, and perhaps deprives himself of lips and an eye. So they slash on till one

gives

gives out, and many have died in this debate. And 'tis by a paſſive valour they ſhew and prove their activity, a ſort of courage too brutal to be applauded by our black hero ; neverthelels he expreſſed his eſteem for them.

In this voyage Cæſar begat ſo good an underſtanding between the Indians and the Engliſh, that there were no more fears or heart-burnings during our ſtay, but we had a perfect, open, and free trade with them. Many things remarkable. and worthy reciting, we met with in this ſhort voyage ; becauſe Cæſar made it his buſineſs to ſearch out and provide for our entertainment, eſpecially to pleaſe his dearly adored Imoinda, who was a ſharer in all our adventures ; we being reſolved to make her chains as eaſy as we could, and to compliment the prince in that manner that moſt obliged him.

As we were coming up again, we met with ſome Indians of ſtrange aſpects ; that is, of a larger ſize. and other ſort of features, than thoſe in our country. Our Indian ſlaves, that rowed us aſked them ſome queſtions ; but they could not

D 3   underſtand

underſtand us but ſhewed us a long cot‑
ton ſtring. with ſeveral knots on it, and
they had been coming from the moun‑
tains ſo many moons as there were knots:
They were habited in ſkins of a ſtrange
beaſt, and brought along with them bags
of gold   which, as well as they
could give us underſtand, came ſtream‑
ing in the ſmall channels down the high
moun   the rains fell ; and of‑
fered   to any body, or per‑
ſons,   to the mountains.
We   men up to Parham,
where   were kept till the lord gover‑
nor came, and becaſe all the people
were mad to be going on this golden ad‑
venture the governor, by his letters,
commanded (for they ſent ſome of the
gold to him,) that a guard ſhould be ſet
at the mouth of the river of Amazons,
(a river ſo called, almoſt as broad as the
river of Thames; and prohibited all peo‑
ple from going up that river. it conduct‑
ing to thoſe mountains of gold.   But we
going of for England. before the project
was further proſecuted, and the gover‑
nor being drowned in a hurricane, either

the

the defign died, or the Dutch have the advantage of it · Ard 'tis to be bemoaned what his Majefty loft, by loofing that part of America

Tho' the digreffion is a litt'e from my ftory, fince it contains fome proofs of the curiofity and daring of this great man, I was content to omit nothing of his character.

It was thus for fome time we diverted him ; but now Imoinda began to fee fhe was with child, and did nothing but figh and weep for the captivity of her lord, herfelf, and the infant yet unborn; and believed, if it were fo hard to gain the liberty of two, it would be more difficult to get that for three. Her griefs were fo many darts in the great heart of Cæfar, and taking his opportunity on Sunday, when all the Whites were over-taken in drink, as there was abundance of feveral trades, and flaves for four years, that inhabited among the Negro houfes ; and Sunday being the day of debauch, (otherwife they were a fort of fpies upon Cæfar) he went, pretending out of goodnefs to them, to feaft among

them

them, and sent all his music, and ordered a great treat for the whole gang, a-
bout three hundred negroes, and about
an hundred and fifty were able to bear
arms, such as they had, which were sufficient to do execution, with spirits accordingly For the English had none but
rusty swords, that no strength could draw
from a scabboard; except the people of
particular quality, who took care to oil
them, and keep them in good order.
The guns also, unless here and there one
of those newly carried from England,
would do no good or harm ; for 'tis the
nature of that country, to rust and eat
up iron. or any metals but gold and silver.   And they are very expert at the
bow, which the Negroes and Indians are
perfect masters of.

Cæsar, having singled out these men
from the women and children, made an
harangue to them, of the miseries and
ignominies of slavery ; counting up all
their toils and sufferings, under such loads
burdens and drudgeries, as were fitter
for beasts than men ; senseless brutes,
than human souls. He told them, it was
not

not for days months or years, but for eternity; there was no end to be of their misfortunes: They suffered not like men, who might find a glory and fortitude in oppreſſion, but like dogs, that loved the whip and bell, and fawned the more they were beaten: That they had loſt the divine quality of men, and were become Inſenſible aſſes, fit only to bear. Nay, worſe; an aſs, or dog, or horſe, having done his duty, could lie down in retreat and riſe to work again, and while he did his duty, endured no ſtripes; but men, villainous ſenſeleſs men, ſuch as they, toiled on all the tedious week 'till black Friday; and then, whether they worked or not, whether they were faulty or meriting they promiſcuouſly, the innocent with the guilty, ſuffered the infamous whip, the ſordid ſtripes, from their fellow-ſlaves, 'till their blood trickled from all parts of their body; blood, whoſe every drop ought to be revenged with a life of ſome of thoſe tyrants that impoſe it. ' And why [ſaid he] my dear friends ' and fellow-ſufferers, ſhould we be ſlaves ' to an unknown people? have they van-

' quiſhed

'quifhed us nobly in fight? Have they
'won us in honourable battle? And are
'we by the chance of war become their
'flaves? This would not anger a noble
'heart; this would not animate a fol-
'dier's foul: No, but we are bought
'and fold like apes or monkies, to be
'the fport of women, fools and cowards;
'and the fupport of rogues and runagades,
'that have abandoned their own coun-
'tries for rapine, murder, theft and vil-
'lanies. Do you not hear every day how
'they upbraid each other with infamy of
'life below the wildeft favages? And
'fhall we render obedience to fuch a de-
'generate race, who have no one human
'virtue left, to diftinguifh them from the
'vileft creatures? Will you, I fay, fuffer
'the lafh from fuch hands?' They all
'reply'd with one accord, 'No, no, no;
'Cæfar has fpoke like a great captain,
'like a great king.

After this he would have proceeded,
but was interrupted by a tall negro, of
fome more quality than the reft, his name
was Tufcan; who bowing at the feet of
Cæfar, cry'd 'My lord, we have liften'd
with

'with joy and attention to what you
'have said; and were we only men, we
'would follow so great a leader
'thro' the world; But O! consider we
'are husbands and parents too, and
'have things more dear to us than life;
'our wives and children, unfit for tra-
'vel in those unpassable woods, moun-
'tains and bogs. We have not only
'difficult lands to overcome, but rivers
'to wade, mountains to climb; and ra-
'venous beasts of prey to encounter.'—
To this Cæsar replied, 'That honour
'was the first principle in nature, that
'was to be obeyed; but as no man
'would pretend to that, without all the
'acts of virtue, compassion, charity, love,
'justice and reason, he found it not in-
'consistent with that, to take equal care
'of their wives and children as they would
'of themselves, and that he did not de-
'design, when he led them to freedom,
'and glorious liberty, that they should
'leave that better part of themselves to
'perish by the hand of the tyrants whip:
'But if there were a woman among 'em
'so degenerate from love and virtue, to

D 6   'choose

'choose slavery before the pursuits of
' her husband, and with the hazard of her
' life, to share with him in his fortunes;
' that such a one ought to be abandoned,
' and left as a prey to the common ene-
' my.'

To which they all agreed—and bowed.
After this, he spoke of the impassable
woods and rivers; and convinced them,
the more danger the more glory. He
told them that he had heard of one Han-
nibal, a great captain, had cut his way
through mountains of solid rocks; and
should a few shrubs oppose them, which
they could fire before them? No, 'twas
a trifling excuse to men resolved to die,
or overcome. As for bogs, they are with
a little labour filled and hardened; and
the rivers could be no obstacle, since they
swam by nature, at least by custom, from
the first hour of their birth: that when
the children were weary, they must carry
them by turns, and the woods and their
own industry would afford them food.—
To this they all assented with joy.

Tuscan then demanded, what he would
do: he said he would towards the sea,

plant

plant a new colony, and defend it by their valour: and when they could find a ship, either driven by stress of weather, or guided by providence that way, they would seize it and make it a prize, till it had transported them to their own countries at least they should be made free in his kingdom, and be esteemed as his fellow-sufferers, and men that had the courage and bravery to attempt. at least for liberty ; and if they died in the attempt, it would be more brave than to live in perpetual slavery.

They bowed and kissed his feet at his resolution, and with one accord vowed to follow him to death ; and that night was appointed to begin their march. They made it known to their wives, and directed them to tie their hamocks about their shoulders, and under their arms like a scarf, and to lead their children that could go, and carry those that could not. The wives who pay an entire obedience to their husbands, obeyed, and stayed for them where they were appointed· The men stayed but to furnish themselves with what defensive arms they could get ; and

all

all met at the rendezvous, where Cæsar made a new encouraging speech to them, and led them out.

But as they could not march far that night, on Monday early, when the overseers went to call them all together to go to work, they were extremely surprized to find not one upon the place, but all fled with what baggage they had You may imagine this news was not only suddenly spread all over the plantation, but soon reached the neighbouring ones; and we had by noon about 600 men, they call the militia of the country, that came to assist us in the pursuit of the fugitives but never did one see so comical an army march forth to war. The men of any fashion would not concern themselves, tho' it were almost the common cause, for such revoltings are very ill examples, and have very fatal consequences oftentimes, in many colonies; but they had a respect for Cæsar, and all hands were against the Parhamites (as they called those of Parham Plantation) because they did not in the first place love the lord-governor: and, secondly, they would have it

that

that Cæfar was ill ufed, and baffled with·
and tis not impoffible but fome of the beft
in the country was of his council in this
flight, and depriving us of all the flaves;
fo that they who were of the better fort
would not meddle in the matter. The
deputy-governor, of whom I have had no
great occafion to fpeak, and who was the
moft fawning fair-tongued fellow in the
world, and one that pretended the moft
friendfhip to Cæfar, was now the only
violent man againft him; and though he
had nothing, and fo need fear nothing,
yet talked and look'd bigger than any man.
He was a fellow, whofe character is fit to
be mentioned with the worft of the flaves:
this fellow would lead his army forth to
meet Cæfar, or rather to purfue him.——
Moft of their arms were of thofe fort of
cruel whips they call cat with nine tails;
fome had rufty ufelefs guns for fhew; o-
thers old bafket hilts, whofe blades had
never feen the light in this age; and o-
thers had long ftaves and clubs. Mr.
Trefry went along with them, rather to
be a mediator than a conqueror in fuch a
battle; for he forefaw and knew if by

D 8   fighting

fighting they put the negroes into difpair they were a fort of fullen fellows, that would drown or kill themfelves before they would yield ; and he advifed that fair means were beft : but Byam was one that bounded in his own wit, and would take his own meafures.

It was not hard to find thefe fugitives; for as they fled they were forced to fire and cut the woods before them : fo that night or day they purfued them by the light they made, and by the path they had cleared. But as foon as Cæfar found he was purfued, he put himfelf into a pof ture of defence, placing all the women and children in the rear ; and himfelf with Tufcan by his fide, or next to him, all promifing to die or conquer. En. couraged thus, they never flood to par ley, but fell on pell-mell upon the Eng- lifh, and killed fome and wounded a great many ; they having recourfe to their whips as the beft of their weapons. And as they obferved no order, they perplexed the enemy fo forely with lafhing them in the eves ; the women and children feeing their hufbands fo treated, being of

fearful

fearful and cowardly difpofitions and hearing the Englifh cry out, Yield, and live !
Yield and be pardoned ! they all ran in
amongft their hufbands and fathers, and
hung about them, crying out, Yield !
yield ! and leave Cæfar to their revenge:
that by degrees they abandoned Cæfar,
and left him only Tufcan and his heroic
Imoinda, who grown as big as fhe was,
did neverthelefs prefs near her lord, having a bow and quiver full of poifon'd arrows, which fhe managed with fuch dex-
terity, that fhe wounded feveral and fhot
the governor into the fhoulder ; of which
wound he had like to have died, but that
an Indian woman, his miftrefs, fucked the
wound and cleanfed it from the venom :
but however, he ftirred not from the place
till he had parly'd with Cæfar, who he
found was refolved to die fighting, and
would not be taken ; no more would
Tufcan or Imoinda. But he, more thirft-
ing after revenge of another fort, than
that of depriving him of life, now made
ufe of all his art of talking and diffembl-
ing, and befought Cæfar to yield himfelf
upon terms which he himfelf fhould pro-

pofe

pofe, and fhould be facredly affented to, and kept by him. He told him, it was not that he any longer feared him, or could believe the force of two men, and a young heroine could overthrow all them, and with all the flaves now on their fide alfo ; but it was the vaft efteem he had for his perfon, the defire he had to ferve fo gallant a man, and to hinder himfelf from the reproach hereafter, of having been the occafion of the death of a prince whofe valour and magnanimity deferved the empire of the world. He protefted to him he looked upon his action as gallant and brave, however tending to the prejudice of his lord and mafter, who would by it have loft fo confiderable a number of flaves ; that this flight of his fhould be looked on as a heat of youth, and a rafhnefs of a too forward courage, and an unconfidered impatience of liberty, and no more ; and that he laboured in vain to accomplifh that which they would effectually perform as foon as any fhip arrived that would touch on his coaft ' So that if he would be pleafed [conti-
' nued he] to furrender yourfelf, all im-
' aginable

' aginable respect shall be paid you ; and
' yourself, your wife and child, if it be
' born here, shall depart free out of our
' land.' But Cæsar would hear of no
composition ; though Byam urged, if he
pursued and went on in his design, he
would inevitably perish, either by great
snakes, wild beasts, or hunger ; and he
ought to have regard for his wife, whose
condition required ease, and not the fa-
tigues of tedious travel, where she could
not be secured from being devoured.—
But Cæsar told him there was no faith in
the white men, or the Gods they adored,
who instructed them in principles so false
that honest men could not live amongst
them ; tho' no people professed so much,
none performed so little : That he knew
what he had to do when he dealt with men
of honour ; but with them a man ought
to be eternally on his guard, and never
to eat and drink with christians, without
his weapon of defence in his hand ; and
for his own security, never to credit one
word they spoke. As for the rashness &
inconsiderateness of his action, he would
confess the governor is in the right ; and
that

that he was afhamed of what he had done in endeavouring to make thofe free, who were by nature flaves, poor wretched rogues, fit to be ufed as chriftians tools, dogs, treacherous and cowardly, fit for fuch mafters ; and they wanted only but to be whipped into the knowledge of the chriftian gods, to be the vileft of all creeping things; to learn to worfhip fuch deities as had not power to make them juft, brave, or honeft: In fine after a thoufand things of this nature, not fit here to be recited, he told Byam, he had rather die, than live upon the earth with fuch dogs. But Trefry and Byam pleaded and protefted together fo much, that Trefry believing the governor to mean what he faid and fpeaking very cordially himfelf, generoufly put himfelf into Cæfar's hands, and took him afide, and perfuaded him even with tears, to live, by furrendering himfelf, and to name his conditions. Cæfar was overcome by his wit and reafons in confideration of Imoinda ; and demanding what he defired, and that it fhould be ratified by their hands in writing, becaufe he had perceived that was the common

way

way of contract between man and man amongst the Whites; all this was performed, and Tuscan's pardon was put in, and they surrendered to the governor, who walked peaceably down into the plantation with them, after giving orders to bury their dead. Cæsar was very much toiled with the bustle of the day, for he had fought like a fury: and what mischief was done he and Tuscan had performed alone; and gave their enemies a fatal proof that they durst do any thing, and feared no mortal force.

But they were no sooner arrived at the place where all the slaves receive their punishments of whipping, but they laid hands on Cæsar and Tuscan, faint with heat and toil: and surprising them, bound them to two several stakes, and whipped them in a most deplorable and inhuman manner, rending the very flesh from their bones, especially Cæsar, who was not perceived to make any moan, or to alter his face, only to roll his eyes on the faithless governor, and those he believed guilty, with fierceness ahd indignation; and to complete his rage, he saw every one of

those

those slaves who but a few days before adored him as something more than mortal, now had a whip to give him some lashes, while he strove not to break his fetters, tho' if he had, it were impossible: but he pronounced a woe and revenge from his eyes, that darted fire, which was at once both aweful and terrible to behold

When they thought they were sufficiently revenged on him, they untied him, almost fainting with loss of blood, from a thousand wounds all over his body; from which they had rent his clothes and led him naked and bleeding as he was and loaded him all over with irons; and then rubbed his wounds, to complete their cruelty, with Indian pepper, which had like to nave made him raving mad; and in this condition, made him so fast to the ground, that he could not stir, if his pains and wounds would have given him leave. They feared Imoinda, and did not let her see this barbarity committed towards her lord, but carried her down to Parham, and shut her up, which was not in kindness to her but for fear she should die

with

with the fight, or mileary the
fhould looie a young flave, and p   p,
the mother.

You muft know, tha when the news
was brought on Monday morning, that
Cæfar had betaken himfelf to the woods,
and carried with him all the Negroes, we
were poffeffed with extreme fear, which
no perfuafions could diffipate, that he
would fecure himfelf till night, and then
would come down and cut all our throats.
This apprehenfion made all us females fly
down the river to be fecured; and while
we were away they acted this cruelty;
for I fuppofe I had authority and intereft
enough there, had I fufpected any fuch
thing, to have prevented it: but we had
not gone many leagues but the news o-
vertook us that Cæfr was taken and whipped like a common flave. We met on
the river with colonel Martin, a man of
great gallantry, wit, and goodnefs, and
whom I have celebrated in a character of
of my new comedy, by his own name,
in memory of fo brave a man: he was
wife and eloquent, and from the finenefs
of his parts, bore a great fway over the
                                    hearts

hearts of the colony : he was a friend to Cæsar, and resented the false dealing with him very much. We carried him back to Parham, thinking to have an accommodation; when we came, the very first news we heard, was that the governor was dead of a wound Imoinda had given him ; but it was not so well. It seems he would have the pleasure of beholding the revenge he took on Cæsar ; and before the cruel ceremony was finished, he dropt down ; and then they perceived the wound he had on his shoulder was by a venomed arrow, which, as I said, his Indian mistress healed, by sucking the wound.

We were no sooner arrived, but we went up to the plantation to see Cæsar; whom we found in a very miserable and unexpressible condition ; and I have a thousand times admired how he lived in such tormenting pain. We said all things to him that trouble, pity, and good-nature could suggest, protesting our innocency of the fact, and our abhorrence of such cruelties ; making a thousand professions and services to him, and begging as many

ny

ny pardons for the offenders, till we faid fo much, that he believed we had no hand in his ill treatment; but told us he could never pardon Byam; as for Trefry he confeffed he faw his grief and forrow for his fuffering, which he could not hinder, but was like to have been beaten down by the very flaves, for fpeaking in his defence: But for Byam, who was their leader, their head——and fhould, by his juftice and honour, have been an example to them——for him he wifhed to live to take a dire revenge of him; and faid, it had been well for him, if he had facrificed me, inftead of giving me the contemptible whip. He refufed to talk much but begging us to give him our hands, he took them, and protefted never to lift up his to do us any harm. He had a great refpect for colonel Martin, and always took his counfel like that of a parent, and affured him, he would obey him in any thing, but his revenge on Byam: There-‘ fore (he faid) for his own fafety, let ‘ him fpeedily difpatch me; for if I could ‘ difpatch myfelf, I would not, 'till that ‘ juftice were done to my injured perfon,

and

and the contempt of a foldier: No, I
' would not kill myfelf, even after a whip-
' ping, but will be content to live with
' that infamy, and be pointed at by every
' grinning flave, till I nave compleated
' my revenge; and then you fhall fee that
' Oroonoko fcorns to live with the indig-
' nity that was put on Cæfar.' All we could
do, could get no more words from him,
and we took care to have him put immediately into a healing bath, to rid him of
his pepper, and ordered a chirurgeon to
anoint him with healing balm, which he
fuffered, and in fome time he began to be
able to walk and eat. We failed not to
vifit him every day, and to that end had
him brought up to an apartment at Parham.

The governor had no fooner recovered
and had heard of the menaces of Cæfar,
but he called his council. who (not to dif-
grace them, or burlefque the government
there) confifted of fuch notorious villains
as Newgate never tranfported; and poffibly originally were fuch who underftood neither the laws of God or man
and had no fort of principles to make
then

them worthy of the name of men; but as the very council table would contradict and fight with one another, and fwear fo bloodily, that 'twas terrible to hear and fee them. Some of them were afterwards hanged, when the Dutch took poffeffion of the place, others fent off in chains.——But calling thefe fpecial rulers of the nation together, and requiring their counfel in this weighty affair, they all concluded that (damn 'em) it might be their own cafes; and that Cæfar ought to be made an example to all the Negroes, to fright them from daring to threaten their betters, their lords and mafters; and at this rate no man was fafe from his own flaves; and concluded, nemine contradicente, that Cæfar fhould be hanged.

Trefry then thought it time to ufe his authority, and told Byam, his command did not extend to his lordfhip's plantation; and that Parham was as much exempt from the law as White-hall; and that they ought no more to touch the fervants of the lord———(who there reprefented the king's perfon) than they could thofe about the king himfelf; and
that

that Parham was a sanctuary; and tho'
his lordship was absent in person, his
power was still in being there, which he
had entrusted with him, as far as the do-
minions of his particular plantations
reached, and all that belonged to it; the
rest of the country, as Byam was lieute-
nant to his lord, he might exercise his
tyranny upon. Trefry had others as
powerful, or more, that interested themselves in Cæsar's life, and absolutely said
he should be defended. So turning the
governor and his wise council out of doors
(for they sat at Parham-house) we set
a guard upon our lodging-place, and
would admit none but those we called
friends to us and Cæsar.

The governor having remained wounded at Parham, till his recovery was compleated, Cæsar did not know but he was
still there, and indeed for the most part,
his time was spent there : for he was one
that loved to live at other people's ex-
pence, and if he were a day absent, he
was ten present there ; and used to play
and walk, and hunt and fish with Cæsar.
So that Cæsar did not at all doubt, if he

once recovered ſtrength, but he ſhould find an opportunity of being revenged on him; though after ſuch a revenge, he could not hope to live: for if he eſcap'd the fury of the Engliſh mobile, who perhaps would have been glad of the occaſion to have killed him, he was reſolved not to ſurvive his whipping; yet he had ſome tender hours, a repenting ſoftneſs, which he called his fits of cowardice, wherein he ſtruggled with love for the victory of his heart, which took part with his charming Imoinda there; but for the moſt part, his time was paſt in melancholy thoughts, and black deſigns. He conſidered, if he ſhould do this deed, and die either in the attempt or after, it left his lovely Imoinda a prey, or at beſt a ſlave to the enraged multitude; his great heart could not endure that thought: Perhaps [ſaid he] ſhe may firſt be raviſh'd by every brute; expoſed firſt to their naſty luſts, and then a ſhameful death: No he could not live a moment under that apprehenſion, too inſupportable to be borne. Theſe were his thoughts and his ſilent arguments with his heart, as he told us.

us afterwards: so that now resolving not only to kill Byam, but all those he thought had enraged him; pleasing his great heart with the fancied slaughter he should make over the face of the plantation, he first resolved on a deed, [that however horrid it first appeared to us all] when we had heard his reasons, we thought it brave and just. Being able to walk, and as he believed, fit for the execution of his great design, he begged Trefry to trust him into the air, believing a walk would do him good; which was granted him; and taking Imoinda with him, as he used to do in his more happy and calmer days, he led her up into a wood, where after a thousand sighs, and long gazing silently on her face, while tears gushed, in spite of him from his eyes; he told her his design, first of killing her, and then his enemies, and next himself, and the impossibility of escaping, and therefore he told her the necessity of dying. He found the heroic wife faster pleading for death, than he was to propose it, when she found his fixed resolution; and on her knees, besought him not to leave her a prey to

his

his enemies. He [grieved to death] yet pleafed at her noble refolution, took her up, and embracing her with all the paf-fion and languifhment of a dying lover, drew his knife to kill this treafure of his foul, this pleafure of his eyes ; while tears trickled down his cheeks, hers were fmiling with joy fhe fhould die by fo noble a hand, and be fent into her own country [for that's their notion of the next world] by him fhe tenderly loved, and fo truly adored in this : For wives have a refpect for their hufbands equal to what any other people pay a deity ; and when a man finds any occafion to quit his wife, if he love her, fhe dies by his hand ; if not, he fells her, or fuffers fome other to kill her. It being thus, you may believe the deed was foon refolved on ; and 'tis not to be doubted, but the part-ing, the eternal leave-taking of two fuch overs. fo greatly born, fo fenfible, fo beautiful, fo young and fo fond, muft be very moving, as the relation of it was to me afterwards.

All

[All that love could say in such cases, being ended, and all the intermitting irresolutions being adjusted, the lovely, young and adored victim, lays herself down before the sacrificer; while he with a hand resolved, and a heart breaking within, gave the fatal stroke, first cutting her throat, then severing her yet smiling face from that delicate body, pregnant as it was with the fruits of tendereft love As soon as he had done, he laid the body decently on leaves and flowers, of which he made a bed, and concealed it under the same coverlid of nature; only her face he left yet bare to look on: But when he found she was dead, and past all retrieve, never more to bless him with her eyes & soft language, his grief swelled up to rage he tore, he raved, he roared like some monster of the wood, calling on the lov'd name of Imoinda. A thousand times he turned the fatal knife that did the deed towards his own heart, with a resolution to go immediately after her ; but dire revenge, which was now a thousand times more fierce in his soul than before, prevents him; and he would cry out, 'No, 'since

"Noble Savage"

' since I have sacrificed Imoinda to my re-
' venge, shall I lose that glory which I
' have purchased so dear, as at the price
' of the fairest, dearest, softest creature
' that ever nature made ? No, no ! ' —
Then at her name grief would get the
ascendant of rage, and he would lie down
by her side, and water her face with
showers of tears, which never were wont
to fall from those eyes ; and however bent
he was on his intended slaughter, he had
not power to stir from the sight of this
dear object, now more beloved, and more
adored than ever.

He remained in this deplorable condition for two days, and never rose from
the ground where he had made her sad sa-
crifice. At last rouzing from her side,
and accusing himself with living too long,
now Imoinda was dead, and that the deaths
of those barbarous enemies were deferred
too long, he resolved now to finish the
great work: but offering to rise, he found
his strength so decay'd, that he reeled to
and fro, like boughs assailed by contrary
winds, so that he was forced to lie down
again, and try to summon all his courage
to

to his aid. He found his brains turned round, and his eyes were dizzy, and objects appeared not the fame to him they were wont to do, his breath was fhort, and all his limbs furprifed with a faintnefs he had never felt before. He had not eat in two days, which was one occafion of his feeblenefs, but excefs of grief was the greateft : yet ftill he hoped he fhould recover vigour to act his defign, and lay expecting it yet fix days longer; ftill mourning over the dead idol of his heart, and ftriving every day to rife, but could not.

In all this time you may believe we were in no little afffliction for Cæfar and his wife ; fome were of opinion he was efcaped, never to return ; others thought fome accident had happened to him : but however, we failed not to fend out a hundred people feveral ways, to fearch for him A party of about forty went that way he took, among whom was Tufcan, who was perfectly reconciled to Byam they had not gone very far into the wood before they fmelt an unufual fmell, as of a dead body, for ftinks muft be very noifome, that can be diftinguifhed among such a quantity of natural sweets, as every inch of that land produces; so that they concluded they should find him dead or somebody that was so; they passed on towards it, as loathsome as it was, and made such a rustling among the leaves that lie thick upon the ground, by continual falling, that Cæsar heard he was approached: and though he had during the space of these eight days, endeavoured to die, but found he wanted strength, yet looking up, and seeing his pursuers, he rose and reeled to a neighbouring tree, against which he fixed his back; and being within a dozen yards of those that advanced and saw him, he called out to them, and bid them approach no nearer, if they would be safe. So they stood still and hardly believing their eyes, that would persuade them that it was Cæsar that spoke to them, so much he was altered; they asked him what he had done with his wife. for they smelt a stink which almost struck them dead? He pointing to the dead body, sighing, cried, 'Behold her here.' they put off the flowers that coved her, with their sticks, and found she

she was killed. and cried out, 'Oh, monster! that hast murdered thy wife.' I 'm
asking him . . . 'e . . . .
He answered . e had no leisure to answer
impertinent questions: 'You may go
' back (continued he, and tell the faith-
' less governor, he may thank fortune,
' that I am breathing my last ; and that
' my arm is too feeble to obey my heart
' in what it had designed him : ' But his
tongue faultering and trembling, he could
scarce end what he was saying. The
English taking advantage by his weakness,
cried, 'Let us take him alive by all means.'
He heard them ; and as if he had reviv'd
from a fainting, or a dream, he cried out
' No, gentlemen, you are deceived; you
' will find no more Cæsars to be whipt,
' no more find a faith in me. feeble as
' you think me, I have strength yet left
' to secure me from a second indignity.
They swore all a-new; and he shook his
head and beheld them with scorn. They
then cried out, 'Who will venture on
' this single man ? Will no-body ?' They
stood all silent, while Cæsar replied, 'Fa-
' tal will be the attempt of the first ad-
                                    venturer

'venturer, let him assure himself,' (and at that word, held a knife up in a menacing posture:) 'Look ye, ye faithless 'crew, said he, 'tis not life I seek, nor 'am I afraid of dying,' (and at that word cut a piece of flesh from his own throat, and threw it at them) 'Yet still I would 'live if I could, till I had perfected my 'revenge. But, oh! it cannot be; I 'feel life gliding from my eyes & heart; 'and if I make not haste, I shall fall a 'victim to the shameful whip.' At that, he ripped up his own belly, and took his bowels and pulled them out, with what strength he could; while some on their knees imploring, besought him to hold his hand. But when they saw him tottering, they cried out, 'Will none ven- 'on him?' A bold Englishman cried, 'Yes, if he were the Devil,' (taking courage when he saw him almost dead) and swearing a horrid oath for his farewell to the world, he rushed on him. Cæsar with his armed hand, met him so furly, as struck him to the heart, and he fell dead at his feet. Tuscan seeing that, cried out, 'I love thee, O Cæsar?' and there-

E

'fore

' fore will not fee thee die, if poffible,'
and running to him, took him in his arms,
but, at the fame time, warding a blow
that Cæfar made at his bofom, he received
it quite through his arm; and Cæfar having not ftrength to pluck the knife forth
tho' he attempted it ; Tufcan neither pulled it out himfelf, nor fuffered it to be
pulled out, but came down with it fticking
in his arm ; and the reafon he gave for
it was, becaufe the air fhould not get into the wound. They put their hands a-
crofs, and carried Cæfar between fix of
them, fainting as he was, and they thought
dead, or juft dying; and they brought
him to Parham, and laid him on a couch
and had the Chirurgeon immediately to
him, who dreft his wounds, and fewed
up his belly, and ufed means to bring
him to life, which they effected. We
ran all to fee him ; and, if before we
thought him fo beautiful a fight, he was
now fo altered, that his face was like a
_____'s head blacked over, nothing but
teeth and eye-holes : for fome days we
_____ no body to fpeak to him, br
_____ to be poured down h
throat

throat; which suftained his life, and in fix or feven days he recovered his fenfes: for, you muft know, that wounds are almoft to a miracle cured in the Indies; unlefs wounds in the legs, which they rarely ever cure.

When he was well enough to fpeak we talked with him, and afked him fome queftions about his wife, and the reafon why he killed her; and he then told us what I have related of that refolution, and of his parting, and he befought us we would let him die, and was extreemly afflicted to think it was poffible he might live · he affured us, if we did not difpatch him, he would prove very fatal to a great many. We faid all we could to make him live, and gave him new affurances; but he begged we would not think fo poorly of him, or of his love Imoinda, to imagine we could flatter him to life again : But the chirurgeon affured him he could not live, and therefore he need not fear. We were all (but Cæfar) afflicted at this news and the fight was ghaftly; his difcourfe was fad; and the earthy fmell about him fo ftrong, that I was perfuaded to leave

the

the place for some time, (being myself but sickly, and very apt to fall into fits of dangerous illness upon any extraordinary melancholy.) The servants and Trefry, and the chirurgeons, promised all to take what possible care they could of the life of Cæsar; and I, taking boat, went with other company to colonel Martin's, about three days journey down the river. But I was no sooner gone, than the governor taking Trefry, about some pretended earnest business, a day's journey up the river, having communicated his design to one Banister, a wild Irishman, one of the council, a fellow of absolute barbarity, and fit to execute any villany, tho' rich; he came up to Parham, and forcibly took Cæsar, and had him carried to the same post where he was whipped; and causing him to be tied to it, and a great fire made before him, he told him he should die like a dog, as he was. Cæsar replied, This was the first piece of bravery that ever Banister did, and he never spoke sense till he pronounced that word; and if he would keep it, he would declare in the other world, that he was the only man of all
all

all the Whites, that ever he heard speak truth. And turning to the men that bound him, he said, he said, ' My friends, am I to die or to be whipt ?' And they cried, ' Whipt ! no, you shall not escape so well.' And then he replied, smiling, ' A blessing on thee ; and assured them they need not tye him, for he would stand fix'd like a rock. and endure death so as should encourage them to die : ' But if you whip me, (said he) be sure you tie me fast.

He had learned to take tobacco ; and when he was assured he should die, he desired they would give him a pipe in his mouth, ready lighted; which they did: and the executioner came, and first cut off his members and threw them into the fire, after that, with an ill-favoured knife, they cut off his ears and his nose, and burned them; he still smoaked on as if nothing had touched him ; then they hacked off one of his arms, and still he bore up and held his pipe ; but on cutting off his other arm, his head sunk, and his pipe dropt and he gave up the ghost, without a groan or a reproach. My mother and sister were by him all the while, but not suf-

fered

fered to fave him ; fo rude and wild were the rabble, and fo inhuman were the juftices who ftood by to fee the execution who after paid dear enough for their in-folence. They cut Cæfar into quarters and fent them to feveral of the chief planta-tions : one quarter was fent to colonel Martin ; who refufed it, and fwore, he had rather fee the quarters of Banifter, and the governor himfelf, than thofe of Cæfar, on his plantations; and that he could govern his Negroes, without terri-fying and grieving them with frightful fpectacles of a mangled king.

Thus died this great man, worthy of a better fate, and a more fublime wit than mine to write his praife: yet I hope the reputation of my pen is confiderable e nough to make his glorious name to fur vive to all ages, with that of the brave the beautiful· and the conftant Imoinda.

F I N I S.

CPSIA information can be obtained
at www.ICGtesting.com
Printed in the USA
LVOW09s1451270817

546569LV00004B/166/P